The following is
received

Many Realtors® might put this down as too elementary, but I wish all my clients would review the simple steps provided here so they could learn to be an effective part of the teamwork it takes to fulfill their dreams. This book has the exact things most buyers and sellers need to know but are afraid to ask.

—John Foltz, President, Realty Executives

This book is a wonderful road map for the ever-confusing world of real estate. It's like having your own personal coach in a box.

—Melissa Giovagnoli, Author, best-selling book, *Networlding: Building Relationships and Opportunities for Success* and *How to Grow a Great Business and Power Network*

The real estate world is constantly changing, so anyone who is even considering buying [or selling] property of any kind should first get a copy of this easy-to-read and straightforward book. [It] demonstrates how valuable a good real estate professional can be—and further—how to select the right one. Smart real estate agents will also read the book to ensure their [clients] are receiving the service and the expertise they deserve.

—Dave Liniger, Co-founder and Chairman of RE/MAX

This book should be required reading for all Realtors® and for anyone serious about real estate.

—Peter J. McLaughlin, author of *CatchFire: A Seven Step Program to Ignite Energy, Defuse Stress and Power Boost Your Performance*

I read your book and I think it is eminently readable. That's one thing most such publications intended for the public fail to be. There is a lot of good information in it that consumers can benefit from.

—Edwin J. Ricketts, Deputy Commissioner of the Arizona Department of Real Estate

. . . In life it seems you don't get what you deserve, you get what you negotiate, and *How to Make Your REALTOR® Get You the Best Deal* gives you the necessary tools it takes to be in the best possible position to negotiate in real estate. My hat is off to Jenny, Ken, and their national consortium.

—Mike Barnett, VP Technology of Internet Crusade (an organization providing communication training to Realtors® nationwide)

In this book . . . profoundly successful real estate agents have provided a simple guide through the often dark and confusing waters of home buying or selling. They demonstrate the impact of recent changes in the law and how those changes can affect the quality of representation one receives. Read this book and you will learn how to screen, select, and then use your Realtor® in a way that *Gets You the Best Deal.*

—Steve Largent, U.S. Congressional Representative, Oklahoma

This is a ground-breaking work for home sellers. It is not only a quick read, but it puts in layman's terms the language of real estate. This book will do more to empower the home seller than anything else in print. I strongly recommend you buy this book before you even consider putting your home on the market.

—Michael E. Houtari, Corporate Attorney

Get the Best Deal When Selling Your Home

Northern Virginia Edition

Get the Best Deal When Selling Your Home

Northern Virginia Edition

by Susan Mekenney
and
Ken Deshaies

Gabriel Publications

Published by:
Gabriel Publications
14340 Addison St. #101
Sherman Oaks, California 91423
(818) 906-2147 Voice
(800) 940-2622 Toll Free
(818) 990-8631 Fax
www.GabrielBooks.com

ISBN 978-1-891689-51-7
ISBN 1-891689-51-7
Library of Congress Catalog Card Number: 2004107221

Distributed by: Partners Book Distributors
Publisher: Gabriel Publications, Simon Rawlinson, V.P.
Editors: David Robman and Kate Shaffar
Typography: SDS Design, info@sds-design.com
Cover Design: Dale Schroeder, SDS Design

Manufactured in the United States of America.

Contents

Section I
Selling Your Home: The Basics

Section II
Buying Your Next Home

Appendices

Acknowledgments by Susan Mekenney

When I was asked by **Ken Deshaies** and **Gabriel Publications** to co-author a second book on real estate, I was flattered beyond belief. It was a little over two years ago that both had approached me to co-author, **How To Make Your Realtor Get You The Best Deal, Virginia Edition**, which turned out to be an amazing experience. I knew at that time this book was an opportunity for me to provide Northern Virginia and my clients with something of real value, and to honor the many people who have mentored, supported and believed in me throughout the years. Thank you, Ken for this fantastic opportunity.

This book is dedicated to my parents, **Joe and Ellie Szollosi**, who instilled in me early on the work ethic that has been with me throughout life.

In addition to my parents, there are numerous people I would like to recognize that have been intimately involved in helping me write this book. Let me start with my husband, **C. Robert**, (a.k.a. Bob) who has never said "no" and, regardless, continues to support me and my efforts. He is my rock.

To all of my clients, many of whom are named in the various testimonials in this book, who have benefited from my services and have taken the time to refer me to their family, friends and business associates because they believed in me. Because of them, my business continues to be 90–95 percent referral.

A special mention to **Lisa Stevens**, my assistant and friend. The house pictured on the front of this book is Lisa's house. I first met Lisa and her husband Michael when I sold them that house. Since then our friendship has grown and Lisa now works with me on a part time basis. She is a daily inspiration to me and the major reason I was able to complete this second book. I couldn't have done it without her.

A special thanks to **Paul Nagel** with **First of America Mortgage**, **Myrna Keplinger** with **The Settlement Group**, **Barbara Dill** with **RE/MAX Allegiance**, and **Jesse Dennehy** with the **Northern Virginia Association of REALTORS®** for their help in researching various aspects of this book.

I would like to acknowledge, **Carmen Hernandez**, who recently gave up her long fight with breast cancer. Carmen was a client as well as a friend and an inspiration to me, and all those individuals she came in contact with. While she will be missed, her spirit will live on forever with those of us who had the pleasure of her company.

My list of thank yous would not be complete without acknowledging, **David Robman**, my motivational production editor, who daily kept me on task.

Lastly to my sons, **Jonathan, Christopher**, and my "adopted" son **Jeff Parker**. I have watched you turn into adults and my love for you still grows daily.

"The big secret in life is that there is no big secret. Whatever your goal, you can get there if you're willing to work."

—Oprah Winfrey

Acknowledgments by Ken Deshaies

There are those without whom this book would not have been written and they deserve more than the recognition given here. Their faith in me, at times, exceeded my own.

My publisher, **Rennie Gabriel**, with whom I have formed a partnership of ideas that has done several things. My first book, *How to Make Your Realtor Get You the Best Deal*, has been much more successful than either of us ever imagined. As a consequence, we have both been able to bring a semblance of understanding and self help to thousands of consumers across this great land. We have also enabled dozens of Realtors® to participate in getting out the message. In the process, we have become great friends and cohorts. Not everyone will agree with our methods, but then, we have not been seeking agreement. What we have done, I would hope, is to empower people on both sides of the real estate purchasing process along with the professionals who work with and represent them.

Davida Sims and **David Robman** contributed so much to this manuscript, and their efforts are more than appreciated.

The hundreds of clients with whom my wife, **Mary** and I have worked with through the years have provided the fodder and the inspiration for this book. So many of them have become good friends in the process that our family is huge in its abundance.

Patricia McDade, founder and inspirational leader of **The Entrepreneurial Edge**, provided the initial kick in the proverbial rear to get me to do that over which I'd procrastinated for so long.

"You don't end up in the grave. You end up in the hearts of the people you have touched."

Disclaimer

We've tried, we really have. We have attempted to ensure that everything said here is accurate and relevant. But laws change, circumstances vary, home prices and interest rates change, and there is always the possibility for error. There may be mistakes, both typographical and in content, and the information was current only up to the printing date. Using the guidance offered here, along with your selection of a competent real estate professional, you should feel confident in purchasing or selling real estate. This text should be used only as a general guide and not as the ultimate source of real estate information. If your situation is complicated by any of a myriad of factors, such as the property being a business, farm or ranch, or if it has soil, septic tank, well, or title problems, we recommend you consult with a Realtor® who specializes in that area. We are not providing any accounting, legal or tax advice in this book. We recommend that you hire an attorney or other appropriate professional who can assist with the specifics involved in any legal or tax matter. The purpose of this book is to educate and entertain. The publisher and authors shall have neither liability nor responsibility to any person or entity with respect to any loss or damage caused, directly or indirectly, by the information contained in this book. If you do not wish to be bound by the above, you may return the book for a full refund.

About gender usage: In order to avoid numerous grammatical messes and to make the reading flow better, we have chosen to make this book as gender neutral as possible. We have used *they* and *their,* even for one person, instead of *he or she, his and hers* and so on.

About the term *Realtor®*: This is a registered trademark of the National Association of REALTORS® (NAR), and anyone who uses that term as part of their professional identity must be a member not only of the NAR, but also of their local and state associations. We always encourage both buyers and sellers to seek out the services of a Realtor® when possible. However, even though we recommend the use of a Realtor®, we know there are many small communities in the country where there are no Realtors®. Often throughout this book we refer to "agent," "licensee," "real estate salesperson," "broker," and so forth. We do this because anyone who holds a real estate sales license must abide by laws, which we will cover in Chapter 11. These laws apply to *all* real estate agents in the United States, not just Realtors®. To make the text easier to read you will see the term *Realtor®* used showing the registration mark and lower case letters after the initial capital *R*. Please see Chapter 2 for a more complete explanation of this designation.

Again, please consult with a professional in your state based on your situation. You can also reach the author directly through the contact information provided near the beginning and end of the book. Feel free to contact the author for a referral to a Realtor® in your area.

Introduction by the Publisher

For many people, their home is the largest investment they will make in their lives. This book is designed to help you, as a homeowner, get the greatest return when you're ready to sell that asset. But right now your house is your home. It is where you shelter yourself from the outside world, where you raise children, and bond with your mate or express your individuality. When it comes time to sell your house (and your home) your thinking has to shift from a personal statement of who you are, or your values, to an investment vehicle that will appeal to the greatest audience. It needs to appeal to the specific demographics of your potential buyer. Remember, the prospective buyer will be comparing your house and home to all the others on the market that fit their needs, wants, and desires.

A small change or addition to your house can add thousands of dollars of profit to you, while spending money in the wrong way can actually cost you thousands more than you spent. You will see many examples in the following pages, but here is one example: If you spent $25,000 on a swimming pool, you would be lucky to get half of it back in the increased value of your home. In addition, you would pay additional property taxes, utility bills, and cleaning and maintenance costs over the life of the swimming pool.

Unfortunately, many people think they can save thousands of dollars by selling a home themselves. The requirements of disclosure when selling a home are getting as complicated as brain surgery. I guess someone in need of brain surgery could save thousands of dollars by reading medical manuals and then attempting to perform the operation themselves, but it would just be silly. Selling a home "by owner" is just as silly. How can the experience of selling one or even a few homes match the experience of a professional who does it day in and day out?

A study conducted by the National Association of REALTORS® determined that people who sold their homes themselves received 21 percent less than comparable homes where the owner used the services of a Realtor®. Another way of looking at this is to recognize that avoiding the services of an agent and saving about 6 percent—or less—on commissions cost 21 percent of the sales price that could have been received.

If you were a homebuyer you might be thinking that you're paying 21 percent more when you buy a home through a Realtor® instead of going directly to an owner. But based on national figures, the initial sale price an owner sets is well above the appropriate market price of comparable homes. In most situations a buyer working directly with a seller, with no agent support, will not know if a home is under- or overpriced. They won't know what inspector to hire to evaluate the integrity of the structure and systems, nor might they understand the responsibilities and liabilities of the other party. In many cases they will not know what forms and wording will provide the best protection if something goes wrong. And there are a host of other items that provide safeguards to both the buyer and the seller that they might not know. This book will cover all of these issues, and more.

In this book Susan Mekenney has teamed up with Ken Deshaies to expose the secrets of how Realtors® are able to get more money for home sellers and sell homes faster than those who attempt to do it for themselves. The authors not only share their own experiences, but have interviewed leading Realtors® from around the country in order to gather the best ideas and practices out there. If you are not already a homeowner but looking to buy your first home, this book can also give you invaluable insights into how to find the right home, finance the purchase, and save thousands of dollars in the process.

About the Authors

Susan McKenney has grown her "by referral" real estate business one client at a time. She believes in the concept of a client for life and focuses her energy on their wants and needs. Over 90 percent of her business is referral based, a true testimonial to the level of service she provides for each and every one of her clients.

Susan became a Realtor® after a successful career in sales and marketing with a Fortune 500 company. In 1994, she decided to delve into real estate full time. The skills she honed as a marketing account manager easily transferred to her new career with RE/MAX Allegiance in Alexandria, Virginia.

Staying current on marketing trends, mortgage rates, real estate laws, and technology in this very dynamic real estate market is an integral part of Susan's daily agenda and something she takes very seriously. In the process, she has earned her Accredited Buyer Representative (ABR), Certified Residential Specialist (CRS), Certified Real Estate Consultant (C-CREC), Internet Certified Professional (e-PRO), Graduate REALTORS® Institute (GRI), and Real Estate in Cyberspace Specialist (RECS) designations, all to better serve her clients.

In May of 2002, Susan challenged herself on a new front by joining the Avon Breast Cancer Team, completing the 3-day, 60-mile walk and learning the true meaning of being focused.

Susan is very active in her local real estate association, NVAR, Northern Virginia Association of Realtors®, and currently serves as an officer. At this writing, she is running for a second term on their board of directors. NVAR is Virginia's largest association boasting over 13,000 members. The state's current Realtor® population is 37,000 members.

She earned her B.A. from The Ohio State University in Columbus. Susan's degree, combined with her five years in Toastmasters International have given her a strong educational foundation for her business.

Susan and her husband of 29 years, Bob, live in Fairfax, Virginia. They have two sons, Jonathan and Christopher. A favorite family pastime is to work together in the kitchen creating new and exciting meals. Her dream is for both of her sons, as well as her husband, to eventually team up with her to take her growing business into the future.

To Reach Susan Mekenney
(800)768-8650
susan@movetovirginia.com
or
see page 145

Ken Deshaies is a real estate broker in Colorado. Ken is an Accredited Buyer Representative (ABR), Certified Residential Specialist (CRS), a graduate of the REALTOR® Institute (GRI), one of the first 500 Realtors® in the country to become a Certified Internet Real Estate Professional (e-PRO500), a Real Estate Cyberspace Specialist (RECS), is an Allen F. Hainge CyberStar™ (an elite group of Realtors® who have proven that they generate a significant portion of their business through the use of current technology), and is EcoBroker™ Certified. He has coauthored over 70 books on real estate. He was named CyberStar™ of the Year for 2002, and elected President of the Summit Association of REALTORS® for 2003. He served on the committee for the Colorado Association of REALTORS® that spearheaded the change in agency laws effective in 2003. Ken serves on the Grievance Committee of the Colorado Association of REALTORS®, and is an iSucceed mentor.

Ken works in partnership with his wife, Mary, in their brokerage, SnowHome Properties. He began his real estate career in Denver in 1992 and has worked in Summit County since 1994. Located an hour west of Denver, Summit County is home to four ski resorts and the highest freshwater sailing lake in the United States. While selling resort real estate is similar in many ways to selling in a metropolitan area, it offers unique problems. For example, since two out of three buyers are buying nonresidential properties, marketed materials, use of the Internet and extensive use of digital photography are essential to a successful marketing plan.

Prior to real estate, Ken owned a private investigations firm for twelve years in Denver, employing and supervising as many as seven investigators and serving for a period as the President of the Professional Private Investigators Association of Colorado. In this work, he conducted numerous investigations into real estate transactions and fraud claims. Many of the stories in this book are based on Ken's experiences, both before and after he became a Realtor®. During much of this time, he was also a member of the Win/Win Business Forum of Denver and was its president for a year and a half.

To Reach Ken Deshaies
Ken@SnowHome.com
or see page 145

Section I

Selling Your Home: The Basics

1. Going It Alone

While experiencing a strong seller's market here in Northern Virginia, houses seemed to be selling themselves. We thought, what the heck, we'll sell our investment property by ourselves and save the real estate commission. How difficult could it be to sell a house?

Our investment property was located about 20 miles from our primary residence and depending on the day and the hour, the journey could easily turn into an hour commute one way. Potential buyers would make appointments and not show up. The sheer act of showing the house was becoming a major investment in time. That's when we decided to hire Susan to help us sell our property.

In addition to relieving us of the showing nightmare, she was able to make suggestions on improving the appearance of the house and found a neighborhood boy who agreed to cut the grass on a weekly basis. Another time saver for us. Thanks to Susan, we were able to sell the house and net a reasonable profit. Her finding us a replacement property was only icing on the cake.

—Larry Mercado and Carmen Hernandez,
Falls Church, Virginia

Many people who are considering selling their home are not sure how to begin the process. Do you try to sell your house yourself, or do you first enlist an agent? And if you do want to try to sell your house on your own, will word get out to that perfect buyer? The bottom line is that no matter which route you take to sell your home, you need to educate yourself as much as possible. In this area, where the economic stakes can be high, knowledge is power. By reading about the following two experiences, you will see what can sometimes happen in the sale of a home, and understand why it pays to become educated. Although the names have been changed, the following stories are real, and may help you decide whether selling your house yourself will really save you money.

First Story

Jack and Lorraine want to sell their home. Jack decides they should sell their home themselves; Lorraine reluctantly agrees. In the language of real estate, these people are referred to as FSBOs (For Sale by Owners). Jack believes their home is worth $500,000, and using a common 6 percent commission rate, he feels he can save $30,000 by selling the home himself.

Jack spends money on newspaper advertising and holds open houses every Sunday, and after six weeks a buyer is interested. Jack and Lorraine are offered $465,000, and decide to take it; it's only $5,000 less than they would have received if they had paid a Realtor®. After four weeks the buyer cannot get loan approval and the deal falls through. Jack wants to keep the buyer's deposit, but after the threat of a lawsuit he refunds it. Jack starts over again.

Ultimately, Jack sells the house for $455,000. After closing costs and expenses to market his house, but not counting time and aggravation, after paying off his $100,000 mortgage, Jack nets $345,000.

Unfortunately, the story doesn't end here. About a year later, Jack and Lorraine were sued by the buyer because it appeared the home was in a flood-control basin, and the required disclosure to the buyer had not been made. Had Jack paid the $30,000 commission to an agent, he ultimately could have saved himself from legal exposure, been protected in the failure of the first sale, and marketed his house to a wider audience; he might even have sold it for the initial asking price of $500,000. So in the end, Jack lost much more than $30,000.

Second Story

Bill and Sara also want to sell their home. Sara convinces Bill that they should work with a Realtor® and they choose Linda Lister. After Linda does comparisons of similar property sales in the area, she determines the home value at $480,000. She then makes recommendations on how to clean the house, rearrange the furniture to make it look more spacious, and otherwise spruce it up with paint, wallpaper, and landscaping. After spending $5,000, Linda feels the home could sell for $500,000, and lists it at $499,000.

Linda handles the advertising, places the house in the Multiple Listing Service (MLS), markets the property to other Realtors® in her office and at other Realtor® meetings, and holds several open houses.

At an open house for other brokers (also known as a Brokers' Open) she is told of a serious buyer who would be a fit for Bill and Sara's house. She follows up and obtains an offer of $485,000. Bill and Sara are on vacation when the offer comes in and handle the paperwork by phone and fax; Linda takes care of the required legal disclosures and, after some back-and-forth negotiation, the home sells for $495,000.

Because of Linda's relationship with a mortgage lender, she is able to help the buyers obtain the loan they need, even though it could have been handled by the buyer's Realtor®. Also, because of her relationship with the escrow company she is able to get reductions in the fees Bill and Sara have to pay.

After commissions, closing costs, and paying their $100,000 mortgage, Bill and Sara receive $360,300, with no aggravation or legal troubles.

As we said in the Introduction, a study conducted by the National Association of REALTORS® determined that people who sold their homes themselves received 21 percent less than comparable homes where the owner used the services of a Realtor®. Sellers who wanted to save paying an agent commission received less than they could have. Buyers have the peace of mind of knowing they purchased a home based on actual comparisons rather than the seller's greed factor, plus all of the other services the Realtor® has to offer. Involving a Realtor® is a win for both the buyer and the seller.

Although these stories are not a guaranteed representation of the realities of selling your own home, what they do illustrate is that you must be educated. And often it pays to rely on an expert's education and experience.

If you do decide that you are prepared for the task of selling your own home, here are some important suggestions:

(1) Take the time to educate yourself about the process of real estate transactions. Know how the process works from beginning to end, and what contractual and legal obligations you will be responsible for.

(2) Know what transactions must be performed by outside professionals, such as inspectors, title agents or attorneys.

(3) Pay to have your house professionally appraised so that you price it correctly. Never rely on what your neighbors said they got for their house or some of the new websites that profess the ability to price your house sight unseen.

(4) Have your home professionally inspected in advance so that you know what might need to be repaired. Take care of the items that you can afford to repair in advance. Remember, once inspected, anything that *hasn't* been repaired/replaced becomes a known material defect, which must be disclosed to a potential buyer by Virginia law.

(5) Establish a marketing budget and determine the best ways to spend it.

(6) Look for a pre-approved rather than a pre-qualified buyer. There will be more on this distinction in the chapter regarding financing.

(7) As a personal safety measure, *never* show your house alone.

Selling your house is not impossible, but it takes diligence, patience, diplomacy, and a willingness to set aside your own biases about your home so that other people's preferences can be understood and accommodated.

Knowing the Process

Before you decide to sell your own home, ask yourself these essential questions to ensure that you are knowledgeable about these important aspects of real estate sales:

✓ Do I know how to properly value my home?

✓ Do I have a marketing strategy to reach the greatest number of potential buyers?

✓ Am I familiar with Virginia's legal requirements for purchase contracts and real estate transfers?

✓ Can I ensure that the buyer is financially able to purchase my home?

- ✓ Do I have the necessary contacts to handle the closing transactions?
- ✓ How are my negotiating skills?
- ✓ Am I prepared to carry back a note if an otherwise qualified buyer does not have the necessary down payment?
- ✓ Am I prepared to give up a partial commission to an agent representing a buyer, or a full commission to a transaction broker or facilitator?

The bottom line is that you must make sure that you are prepared to deal with this major transaction. You should have a plan in place and you should know who can help you with aspects that you can't do alone. Just as money doesn't grow on trees, houses don't sell on their own. If you are selling your house yourself, you must be prepared to make a substantial investment of time. If you are not sure how to handle this complicated sales transaction, using a professional may save you a great deal of unnecessary complications and may still net you more money at the end of the day. Then if you really are prepared, no matter whether you have help or not, you should be able to successfully sell your home.

2. Using a Real Estate Agent

From the minute she walked through our door, we knew things were going to be different with Susan. She stood out above the crowd by not 'telling' us anything. Instead, she 'listened' to our wants and needs. She didn't tell us what price to list our house or to neutralize it by removing our most treasured peach and silver flowered wallpaper. Instead, she walked through our house with us and asked us what we liked most about it and how it differed from all the other homes in our neighborhood. We ended up selling our house for about $7,000 more than the next highest sale in the neighborhood the first week it was on the market!

We would highly recommend using Susan. She believes in building her business by focusing on the wants and needs of her clients. She embraces the philosophy of clients for life and has earned that position with us.

—Harry S. and Mabel L. Truman,
San Antonio, Texas

A real estate agent and a Realtor® are not the same thing. Both may be experienced in the industry, but a Realtor® is a member of the National Association of REALTORS®, and follows a specific code of ethics. (You will find more information on this in the following section, "Credentials.") Anyone who passes their state's real estate licensing exam can become an agent. They may also be referred to as a licensee or real estate salesperson in other parts of the book. There are no cost differences between hiring an agent and a Realtor®.

Although there are some costs associated with enlisting an agent or Realtor®, there are also substantial benefits. For instance, not only do Realtors® have access to thousands of potential buyers that a homeowner may not be aware of, but they also have the knowledge to make sure that you are protected both financially and legally. Additionally, there is some element of risk involved in selling your home, besides the obvious economic one. Realtors® know important legal disclosure requirements. Agents are well aware of the fact that you are allowing complete strangers into your home, and therefore know what precautions you should take to protect both your family and your possessions. But these are just a few of the reasons why enlisting the help of a Realtor® is a good investment. A Realtor® can:

- ✓ Use extensive data and professional experience to assist in determining the best asking price for your home.
- ✓ Provide information about your home to thousands of potential buyers and their agents.
- ✓ Screen buyers and negotiate an offer and a purchase and sale agreement.
- ✓ Take on potential legal obligations and risks.
- ✓ Take you through every step of the process, all the way to closing.

What to Look For

Credentials

Picking an agent is a business decision that should be made with the same deliberation as any other important financial decision. You will want an agent who knows your market, who is experienced, and who you are confident will work hard for you. You've probably noticed that when we've used the term Realtor® in this book, it is capitalized and the registration mark is used. There is a reason for that. The term Realtor® is a trademark of the National Association of REALTORS® (NAR), and anyone who uses that term as part of their professional identity must be a member, not only of NAR but also of their state and local associations. Anyone who is not a member, but is legitimately working in the real estate profession, is still licensed by their state real estate commission and can be identified as an agent, a real estate salesperson, a real estate broker, and so on.

When Realtor® is used, however, it means several things. NAR members have training available only to members. They have the benefit of local meetings and state and national conferences where they can network with other Realtors®. Many deals are actually made for buyers and sellers at those events.

There is a price to pay: Members subscribe to a code of ethics, which commits them to conduct their business with a sense of fair play. The public has some recourse (other than through the legal system) when they feel they have been lied to, mistreated or cheated. They can file an ethics complaint with the local association requesting that a Realtor® be disciplined, or request arbitration if they feel they have actually been cheated out of money. The Grievance Committee and the Professional Standards Committee of the organization handle these complaints. A member is always bound to submit to the grievance process when a complaint is initiated by a buyer or seller.

Members have to pay dues, and the Multiple Listing Service (MLS) charges other fees to maintain a membership in good standing, but the bottom line is that they are in a position to provide much better service to you than nonmembers.

Those who do not have the Realtor® designation operate independently. They often do not do enough business to justify the costs involved in belonging to the NAR. While not always the case, many are retired from other professions or otherwise part time in this profession, so they are not bound by a code of ethics that governs their professional actions, and in some areas they do not have the benefit of MLS access.

So for starters, choose a Realtor®. You'll usually find the designation on their business card.

History

If you were taking in a roommate or boarder, you would screen that person to see if you were compatible. If you were renting out property, you would take a rental application and check out the renter's references and credit history. If you were going into business with or hiring someone, you would be smart to conduct a background check. It never hurts to know who you are working with. The same is true with a real estate agent.

As consumers, we have a terrible history of picking professionals—doctors, lawyers and, yes, real estate agents. We get a referral from a friend, attend the appointment, and that's usually as far as we go. If we end up dissatisfied later, it's our own fault for not taking responsibility for our own selection. We need to prescreen, ask questions, get a feel for how compatible we might be, and determine how well that professional can meet our needs.

If you have a friend in the business, it can be difficult to select someone else, but it might be the most valuable decision you can make. We have known people who listed their homes with friends who specialized in commercial sales but had never sold a house. You need to ask some questions before starting with any real estate agent.

You want to make sure that they are the right person to represent you.

Get a Full-Time Agent or a Professional Team

Most full-time agents work 50 to 60 hours a week or more. They are committed to their work and to their clients. A part-time agent is there to make a deal when it comes along, but either doesn't need the income a full-time career produces, or isn't making it yet, and may hold two or more jobs. Your Realtor® should be available and easy to get in contact with during normal business hours.

Similarly, real estate agents will either have teams with specialists handling different parts of the transaction, or partners who will cover their business while they are away. You will almost always have someone available to provide seamless service. This can be especially beneficial if your Realtor® is on vacation or busy attending to other clients needs.

Questions to ask:

✓ What other type of work do you do?

✓ Do you work full time in real estate?

✓ How flexible is your schedule?

✓ How available are you to show properties on weekdays, weekends, mornings, evenings?

Get an Agent Who Is Busy

Ask your potential agent how many sides (a *side* is one side of the sale) they closed last year and the year before. When one Realtor® has a listing and another one brings in the buyer, each produces one side. An agent who has closed only four to eight sides in a year is not doing enough business to merit having yours. Either they need money, just got started or can't get enough business to survive and are on their way into another profession. An agent who has done 10 or 15 sides is not making a great deal of money but is surviving and probably growing, and believe it or not, they're far above the national average.

An agent who is doing 30 or more sides a year is very busy—usually for a reason. They have attracted business, hopefully because they have served people well, although some Realtors® generate lots of business simply through smart advertising. It is, therefore, important to get a sense of how many transactions were results of referrals from past clients and how satisfied those clients were with the level of service they received from the agent.

Questions to ask:

✓ How many sides did you close last year?

✓ Is that usual for you?

✓ How many sides did you close the year before?

Now that you know how busy the agent is, ask how many of those sides were working with sellers and how many were representing buyers.

Questions to ask:

✓ What percent of your business comes from representing sellers?

✓ How much of your business comes from referrals?

✓ May I speak with five of your most recent sellers?

Check out the Agent's Specialty

If you are selling a home, select an agent who specializes in residential sales. If you want to buy an apartment building or a business, select someone who specializes in commercial sales. There are numerous specialties in real estate, and your agent's specialty should be consistent with your goals. Note that in larger metropolitan areas, like Northern Virginia, Realtors® also tend to specialize in geographic areas, in price ranges or with types of buyers.

An agent who primarily sells million-dollar homes won't have the time or desire for a $350,000 home.

Questions to ask:

✓ Do you have a specialty?

✓ What are the price ranges of the homes you market?

✓ What area/region do you specialize in?

✓ Do you sell commercial and residential real estate?

Make Sure the Agent Is Technologically Current

In today's world, it is vitally important to work with professionals who are computer literate and have a grasp on the new gadgets designed to improve service to their customers. What does that mean?

First, many states require Realtors® to use certain forms in real estate transactions. These forms are almost always available on computer programs, which presents the quickest, most accurate way to generate contracts or offers to purchase. Those who continue to write their contracts by hand or use a typewriter to fill in the blanks on standard forms are living in the past, demonstrating an unwillingness to keep up with the times; they may not be capable of providing the best service.

Other types of software allow Realtors® to track their customers' needs, access increasingly more sophisticated MLS systems, and communicate by email. Digital cameras allow photos and virtual tours of your home complete with interior and exterior views.

If the real estate agent you are interviewing is not able to utilize a computer, beat a hasty retreat. Make sure when an agent says they're computerized, they don't just rely on an assistant or a shared secretary to do all the computer work for them. Your house should have as much Internet exposure as possible. Your wonderful home could be passed over while a competing house that is visible on the Internet is quickly snatched up.

Questions to ask:

✓ Can I have your email address?

✓ What is the address of your website? Do you have more than one?

✓ Will you take digital pictures of my home? How many pictures will appear in the MLS, or in other marketing materials? Will you create a virtual tour of my home?

✓ What other types of advertising do you routinely do?

✓ Can you show me samples of your listings, flyers, ads, and websites?

✓ What is your marketing plan?

✓ What other technology do you use in your business?

Training

Anyone worth their salt in any profession continues to update their knowledge about the work they do. Doctors, lawyers, and mechanics face an ever-changing world when it comes to their professions and must take classes to continue to be of service to their customers. The same is true of Realtors®.

In Virginia, state law requires continuing education classes as follows:

- All brokers and salespeople (licensed prior to January 1, 2004) must complete 16 hours of continuing education (CE) training in order to renew their license every two years. The curriculum includes eight hours of mandatory topics (agency, contracts, ethics, fair housing, and legal updates) and eight hours of elective real estate courses.

- New agents (licensed after January 1, 2004) must complete 30 hours of post licensing (PL) training in order to renew their license for the first time. The curriculum includes 15 hours of mandatory topics (agency law, ethics, fair housing, offer to purchase, and real estate law) and 15 hours of elective real estate courses.

- Associate broker. This demonstrates the real estate professional's commitment to furthering their educational training as well as their commitment to the business. The requirements for a real estate broker's license in Virginia include being at least 18 years of age and having successfully completed 180 hours of approved real estate broker pre-licensing courses. The applicant needs to provide proof of having been actively engaged as a salesperson for 36 of the preceding 48 months.

Good Realtors® find the time to take even more training. There are a number of designations denoting certain continuing education landmarks, which are often signified on business cards as acronyms following the name. While some may be in areas not related to residential sales, all show a commitment on behalf of the Realtor® to keep their professional skills honed, and that's good. Do not work with someone who demonstrates no interest in continuing education. Look for some of the following designations on your prospective agent's business card:

GRI—Graduate, REALTOR® Institute—represents approximately 90 hours of advanced education beyond the training that is required to be licensed. It is usually the first step to becoming more informed and professional.

CRS—Certified Residential Specialist—is the "graduate degree" in residential sales. It requires significant real estate experience coupled with rigorous educational requirements. The average Realtor® takes several years to satisfy those requirements and it usually costs them anywhere from $5,000 to $10,000 in tuition and travel costs. Every **CRS** designee is required to maintain membership in NAR and to abide by its strict code of ethics. Less than 4 percent of all licensed Realtors® hold this designation. Graduates are members of the Residential Sales Council (RSC) and receive continuing information in a variety of ways to keep them abreast of new issues in the area.

ALC—Accredited Land Counselor—similar to a CRS, this usually requires several years and several thousand dollars to achieve. It's the "graduate degree" of land sales.

CCIM—Certified Commercial Investment Member—this designates an expert in commercial property sales, like shopping centers and industrial, office, and apartment buildings. It requires extensive continuing education and graduates are members of the Commercial Sales Council.

e-PRO—Certified Internet Real Estate Professional—this is the only certification program of its kind recognized nationwide and endorsed by the National Association of REALTORS®. Those searching for a Realtor® can have confidence that e-PRO graduates are savvy with all aspects of the Internet. They not only take Internet-empowered consumers seriously, they are also able to meet their online needs.

CyberStar™—An Allen F. Hainge CyberStar™ is one of an elite group of Realtors® from around the country and abroad who have proven efficiency in the use of technology and have agreed to serve as teaching professionals with Allen. They work well with people on the Internet, with email and yes, in person. They are top producers in their markets, and they have exclusive territories. Their websites are often very innovative and provide local information as well.

EcoBroker™ Certified—The EcoBroker™ certification requires completion of a course of study on health hazards in homes, remediation services and resources, energy efficiency, and alternative energy systems. An EcoBroker™ affiliate can boast that 25 percent or more of its agents are EcoBroker™ Certified.

There are many other designations. If you see one you are not familiar with, ask about it. Most professionals are proud of their designations and happy to talk about them. After all, they have spent both time and money in making themselves better able to serve you.

What Is an EcoBroker™?

EcoBroker™ International is a company that trains Realtors® in the advantages of educating both homebuyers and sellers about healthy and energy-efficient homes. The course of instruction takes an agent through health hazards of homes, such as mold, radon, dirty air ducts, and other unhealthy conditions, and helps them understand what mitigation sources are available so this can be shared with their clients. It also covers a variety of energy efficient features that tend to make a home more valuable (based on the premise that lower energy costs will make a home more valuable in the market—and more comfortable to live in). Alternative energy systems are also explored.

There are numerous national, state and local organizations that support and provide information on energy efficiency in homes. The LEED (Leadership in Energy and Environmental Design) Green Building Rating System® is a voluntary, consensus-based national standard for developing high-performance, sustainable buildings. Built Green is a term used by numerous private organizations. The Colorado organization has one of the easier to use checklists. It is a handy guide for homebuilders, sellers and buyers on what to look for in a home. You can access and download the Built Green Checklist at www.BuiltGreen.org. Energy Star is a government organization that not only provides a similar checklist—qualifying for an Energy Star rating is more difficult than Built Green—but it also tests and qualifies home appliances and building materials so that you can know what to buy and know in advance of your purchase what approximate savings you can realize. Check out the requirements, the qualifying appliances, and a variety of other information on energy efficiency at www.EnergyStar.gov.

A Realtor® who is EcoBroker™ Certified is better able to help you understand (a) if your home already has energy efficiency that should be featured in any marketing, and (b) what steps you might take to make your home more energy efficient. If you check the Built Green Checklist at the website above, you will note than many features are simple to implement and may cost relatively little in comparison to the additional dollars the changes could bring in a sale.

For example, you do not need to convert a forced air heating system to solar, or even in-floor radiant, although such changes may, in fact, make a nice difference in the home. But, simply having the integrity of the air ducts tested, and having them cleaned presents a point that can be explained in marketing materials. It becomes a more efficient and healthier system.

It should be noted that the EcoBroker™ certification course is relatively new, so finding a certified EcoBroker™ will be impossible in most areas of the country at this writing. But, if you do find one, be sure that the added knowledge could enhance your agent's ability to help you. You can go to the EcoBroker™ website at *www.EcoBroker.com* to see if there is an agent who is EcoBroker™ Certified near you.

There are many other designations. If you see one you are not familiar with, ask about it. Most professionals are proud of their designations and happy to talk about them.

Attitude

We just cannot end this section without a discussion about attitude and disposition. A good, winning attitude makes up for a lot. We'd much rather work with a newly licensed agent who really wants to help than some old curmudgeon who has been in the profession for years, thinks they have all the answers, and won't listen to anything new. There are a lot of worn-out real estate agents who have "seen it all" still occupying desk space in offices across the country.

Your initial interview with a prospective agent will tell you a lot about their approach to life. Work with an optimist, not a pessimist. Listen to their answers to your questions. Are they saying, "Your house is going to be hard to sell," or "It might be difficult to find the right buyer, but I know that the right exposure can get your house sold."

It isn't brain surgery to figure this out; look for a good, positive attitude as part of your evaluation process.

Agency—Liability

So that you can understand how representation works, it is important to discuss the concept of agency. It's easy to bandy about words like *sub-agency* and *real estate agency*, but the fact of the matter is that *agency* is a legal term. Its use confers a legal obligation and some legal liability.

Let's say, for example, your parents are going to be away on vacation for an extended period of time. While they are gone, they want someone to deposit their checks, pay their bills, and carry on business for them as usual. What they want, in fact, is someone to keep their best interests in mind and to act accordingly. They ask you to represent them, to handle the paperwork in their absence. In order for you to legally perform those functions on their behalf, they would have to sign a document giving you power to act for them in those matters. This document is called a *power of attorney,* and it makes you their legal representative. The person giving the power is known as the *principal,* while the individual who has been given the power is known as the *agent.*

If you were to call your parents' banker in their absence and ask to transfer money from one account to another, the banker would refuse—unless you can prove you are the agent of your parents. In order to do that, you would have to provide their banker with a copy of the power of attorney.

It is also important to understand that a person empowered to be an agent may be in a better position to handle the principal's business than is the principal. The agent is either physically in a better location to handle business for the principal, or is more knowledgeable about the matters to be handled than the principal.

Vicarious Liability

An important aspect of agency to be familiar with is *vicarious liability.* Most people understand that a liability is a risk; it's an exposure. You take on the possibility of a liability when you hire or authorize a person to take actions on your behalf. You are still liable (pursuant to a specific power of attorney for the transaction at hand) for that individual's actions. Your child could damage the property of another, and you might be held responsible for reparations. That is *vicarious liability.* It is extending your risk through reliance on, or responsibility for, others.

In real estate transactions, every time you engage a real estate agent to represent you, you take on some vicarious liability if they act negligibly or unethically on your behalf within the scope of their authority. You rely on your agent to analyze a situation, make and give expert advice, and make recommendations on your behalf that are in your best interest. You have also engaged that agent because you believe their knowledge in this area is greater than yours.

When you engage a Realtor® to represent you, it will behoove you to ensure your agent is experienced, knowledgeable, professional, and willing and able to work for you. Virginia state law requires real estate licensees who are acting as agents of sellers or buyers of property, to advise the potential sellers or buyers with whom they work as to the nature of their agency relationship, along with the rights and obligations it creates. See Disclosure below.

Seller's Agency

When you list your home for sale, you employ the real estate company through your agent as a seller's representative. An agent can provide valuable services to a buyer, but all agents and sub-agents involved in the transaction work on behalf of, and in the best interest of, the seller. A sub-agent may work in a different real estate office. This is the most traditional arrangement in real estate brokerage transactions.

The Virginia agency statute establishes specific duties for a licensee who is in an agency relationship with a seller, buyer, landlord or tenant. These statutory duties for a client require licensees to:

(1) Perform according to the terms of the brokerage relationship;

(2) Promote the best interest of the client, including disclosure;

(3) Maintain *confidentiality*;

(4) Exercise ordinary care and undivided loyalty;

(5) Comply with all applicable laws.

A seller's agent has, without limitation, the following fiduciary duties to the seller: reasonable care, undivided loyalty, confidentiality, full disclosure, obedience, and a duty to account.

The obligations of a seller's agent are also subject to any specific provisions set forth in an agreement between the agent and the seller. In dealings with the buyer, a seller's agent should (a) exercise reasonable skill and care in performance of their duties; (b) deal honestly, fairly, and in good faith; and (c) disclose all facts known to the agent materially affecting the value or desirability of property, except as otherwise provided by law.

The buyer should understand that the selling agent is representing the seller unless the buyer has executed a buyer agency contract or disclosure acknowledgment. The buyer should not make confidential disclosures and should not rely on the selling agent in a way that would strain the sub-agency relationship that may exist. The agent with whom you are working is obligated to discuss this with you at your first meaningful meeting. The agent is required to disclose which party they represent.

Buyer's Agency

If you are buying a home, you can work with an agent as a buyer's agent. A buyer agency relationship exists when the agent represents the buyer exclusively in the real estate transaction. The agent works on behalf of, and in the best interest of, the buyer. This concept may seem new, yet it has been in existence for many years.

If you are a buyer and choose to work with a buyer's agent, you will be asked to sign a buyer agency agreement that must outline the duties to both parties, the duration of contract, any fees (what fees will be earned, who pays, and when), and any other duties required by the parties.

A buyer's agent has, without limitation, the same duties as listed above in the Seller's Agency section. The obligations of a buyer's agent are also subject to any specific provisions set forth in an agreement between the agent and the buyer.

In dealing with the seller, a buyer's agent should (a) exercise reasonable skill and care in performance of the agent's duties; (b) deal honestly, fairly, and in good faith; and (c) disclose all the facts known to the agent materially affecting the buyer's ability and/or willingness to perform a contract to acquire a seller's property that are not inconsistent with the agent's fiduciary duties to the buyer.

Dual Agency

This is not a new term, but its use poses a hurdle many feel is impossible to overcome. Dual agency exists whenever the same real estate firm represents both the buyer and seller. It requires the broker to simultaneously be an agent and advocate for both the buyer and seller in the same transaction. Obviously, this can create conflicting allegiances. When an agent with one realty company represents a seller and an agent in another company represents a buyer, there's little conflict. When you sign a contract with a Realtor®, you are actually retaining the agent's entire company to represent you in your purchase or sale.

In theory, a dual agent owes both the buyer and seller the same fiduciary duties as listed above in the Seller's Agency section. By consenting to dual agency, the conflicting duties to buyer and seller are reconciled and instead the dual agent is required to act with fairness to each party. In addition, most of the other fiduciary obligations are affected because of the contrasting motivations of buyer and seller, who have agreed that the consensual dual agency will not favor the interests of one over those of another.

In a dual agency relationship, your agent cannot give undivided loyalty to either side. The agent must simply present the facts and information within their knowledge and insist the buyer and seller make their own decisions, without pressure from an agent.

In Virginia, dual representation is permitted only when disclosed, and with the knowledge and written consent of both parties. Dual agents function more as facilitators rather than representatives to both parties. The job of a dual agent is to bring parties together to find mutually beneficial solutions to the buyer and sellers' individual needs.

Additionally, in order to protect the interest of all parties, Virginia has created a type of agency called **designated agency**. Designated representative status can arise by choice or by chance. It arises by choice when one company represents both sides, but the parties ask to have the job split between two separate agents. It arises by chance when two agents in the same company are on either side of the transaction by coincidence. In either case, the real estate firm will designate an agent to represent the seller and another to represent the buyer. In no situation can the broker designate himself, because the broker would be considered a dual agent.

With either dual or designated agency, the agent must keep confidential what they are told in confidence unless they have been given written authorization to release the information or the disclosure is required by a specific law. It is the obligation of the agent to treat all parties honestly and not to give the buyer false information.

There Are Advantages to Dual Agency

As much as we feel dual agency is harmful to consumers, it does have some advantages. If you are dealing with only one firm, and especially if there is only one individual agent involved, your lines of communication are shorter. For example, if you ask your agent a question that requires input from the other party, you are likely to get a faster answer, as there is one less firm in the chain of communication.

To protect yourself, discuss the firm's agency policy in your initial contact with them, and ask them to explain how and if they deal with dual agency. Of course, the agent you choose will also have to be experienced and competent in the rest of the skills needed to serve you, which we will address in other areas of this book.

Non-Agency

Some states have embraced an alternative to dual agency: non-agency. In a non-agency relationship, the firm has no fiduciary responsibilities to either party. This arrangement is unattractive to consumers for the obvious reason: There are very few circumstances in which you would hire a firm that has no responsibility to you, and possibly no liability if they damage you. We recommend you strongly consider your options as non-agency affords you the least amount of representation.

In Virginia, non-agency is called Independent Contractor for Services. To date, it has not caught on here. It is commonly misunderstood, and some people mistakenly believe, that the term non-agency referred to anyone who did not have a real estate license. Big problems occur when an agent tries to talk their broker into compensating unlicensed third parties. The listing agreement does not create an exception to the state licensing regulations regarding the improper brokerage of a commission to an unlicensed third-party to a transaction.

Disclosure

In the past, it was up to the seller to inquire about the types of relationships they could have with a broker and what each meant. Most states recognized that this was impractical. How could an unsophisticated consumer be knowledgeable in real estate agency when even most brokers were not? A majority of states eventually shifted the obligation of disclosure to the broker. Presently, the law requires an agent to inform their seller or buyer about the different agency relationships upon the first substantive contact.

Specifically, Virginia state law requires that once an agent is having a substantive discussion about a specific property or properties with an actual or prospective buyer or seller who is not their client and who is not represented by another agent, that agent shall disclose any broker relationship they have with another party to the transaction. In addition, such disclosure must be made in writing at the earliest practical time, but in no event later than the time when specific real estate assistance is first provided. Such disclosure may be given in combination with other disclosures or provided with other information, but if so, the disclosure must be conspicuous, printed in bold lettering, all capitals, underlined, or within a separate box. This disclosure requirement includes open houses. Agents holding a client's home open must disclose their agency relationship to open house guests before discussing the property. It is not unusual to see a sign next to the open house registration log indicating that the host agent is representing the seller.

You must be an educated consumer. When interviewing potential Realtors® to represent you as either a seller's or buyer's agent, if that Realtor® fails to discuss the various choices set forth above, you may wish to reconsider your decision to employ that individual. The agent may be unaware of the law, or is intentionally not informing you of your choices. In either case, they may be doing you a disservice.

Types of Listing Agreements

If you are seeking an agent to help you in the process of selling your home, there are several routes that you can take depending upon the kind of service that you want. Whether you are selling your house on your own or want exclusive representation by a real estate agent to sell your home, you will most likely sign some kind of listing agreement. Face it, real estate agents have access to buyers and can sell your home much more quickly by pooling all their resources than you can with just a "For Sale" sign on your front lawn. Below are some of your options when signing a listing agreement, ranging from the *exclusive right to sell* to a *one-time show.*

Exclusive Right to Sell

If you are looking for the best representation and the widest market through which to sell (remember, the more potential buyers who see your home, the more competitive your price can get), an exclusive right to sell agreement with an agent you trust is the best option you have. With this kind of agreement, you work with one listing agent who will market your home through every channel. They will place your home in the Multiple Listing Service (MLS), market your home to other agents representing buyers, and possibly hold open houses to find potential buyers.

With this kind of listing agreement, you will get the full array of services from your Realtor®, while your Realtor® is guaranteed a commission when your home sells regardless of who brings in the buyer. However, this does not mean that your agent will be the only agent involved in the transaction. While an agent can certainly bring in one of their own buyers, an agent's most powerful marketing tool is networking with a whole array of agents who are representing clients interested in buying your home. This kind of arrangement can get your house the most exposure and hopefully the most competitive price, and you'll end up with the best deal.

An exclusive right to sell agreement is the most common type of listing because of the services it provides and because the agent is guaranteed a commission when your house sells. Therefore, the agent will be appropriately compensated for the amount of time, money, and expertise that goes into the sale of your home.

Open Listing

If you are selling your house on your own but are still willing to work with an agent to bring in a buyer, an open listing is what is most commonly used. In an open listing, a real estate agent representing a buyer has the ability to show your home to their client if it suits the client's needs. If their client buys the home, the agent earns a commission.

There is nothing exclusive about this type of agreement and a seller can offer such listings to any agent who is interested. The only reason that an agent would show your home is because they have a particular buyer in mind who's criteria is a convenient match for your home. Therefore, in an open listing, no agent will bother to market your home or place it in the MLS because they will only earn a commission through a buyer that they bring in. In Northern Virginia, the regional MLS, the Metropolitan Regional Information Systems (MRIS), will not allow such a listing to be placed in the system.

One-Time Show

A one-time show listing is similar to an open listing. With a one-time show listing, the seller is not represented by an agent but allows an agent to bring in one of their buyers and receive a commission. If you are selling your home on your own, and an agent brings in one of their clients, they might ask you to sign a one-time show listing. In this case, the agent bringing in the buyer is guaranteed a commission should their buyer purchase your home.

Like an open listing, your home won't be marketed or placed on the MLS. You will simply have to wait until an agent has a buyer who is interested in your home.

Exclusive Agency Listing

An exclusive agency listing is similar to an exclusive right to sell except the agent listing your home is not guaranteed a commission. For this reason, there are very few agents who will sign this type of listing agreement and, in the end, both you and your agent can end up losing. In an exclusive agency listing, an agent is allowed to list and market your home and will get a commission if they sell your home through any real estate agent or company. However, the seller is also able to find their own buyer, and if they do, the agent does not get any commission despite the fact that they put work into marketing your home. For this reason, many agents who sign an exclusive agency listing will not market your home because they are not guaranteed a commission for time and money spent. Most likely, an agent will just place your home in the MLS and see what happens.

Modified Listing

A modified listing is an exclusive right to sell or exclusive agency listing containing significant modifications to that agreement. These modifications could include such things as an exclusion of a specific purchaser, an exclusion of a specific brokerage firm or a variable rate commission. Regarding the variable rate commission, this could include the listing agent agreeing to a lower rate of commission if that agent sold the property themselves without the cooperation of another real estate agent. The downside of such a listing agreement, especially in a strong seller's market, is the fact that cooperating brokers may refuse to show the property because they feel they are at a competitive disadvantage given the commission arrangement with the listing broker and the seller.

Commissions

Commissions in this country have historically been paid out of the proceeds of the sale, so it has been presumed that the seller actually pays those commissions; however, this is not entirely true. Some professionals believe that because it is the buyer who actually brings the money to the transaction, the buyer pays the commission.

In addition, new agency laws have started to change this tradition by stating that any party to a transaction may pay any broker's compensation, without creating or terminating any agency relationship within that transaction. And more importantly, home values in this country are established with real estate commissions factored in, because home sales have been, and almost always are, handled by real estate agents. The cost of that handling becomes part of the ultimate sale price and value of the home. Therefore, it becomes a moot point who pays the commission—it is simply part of the home value, paid out of the proceeds of the sale. Please be aware that listing commission amounts or percentages are negotiable, and the form of commission agreed to may vary as well. There is no "standard" or "normal" commission.

One thing to be aware of is that agents are not allowed to charge you any fee on top of their commission unless it is explicitly stated in the contract. Hopefully you will select a professional Realtor® and therefore avoid these excess charges, but it is always important to know your rights before you enlist any personal representative.

The bottom line is that you should not let the dollar amount of a Realtor®'s commission scare you away. It is an invaluable investment and can be negotiable. Just as in many complex transactions, expertise costs money, but it is usually well worth the price.

The Discounters

We have taken many property listings after they have been on the market anywhere from three months to a year or so with a discount broker. What are discount brokers? Well, we believe they are often the ones who provide "discount services" and who don't spend much money or effort getting exposure for your property. But they are also the ones who *advertise* that they will charge you less than anyone else. There are often a couple of problems associated with such listings. Once the property has spent sufficient time on the market without a sale, even if it has been priced properly, it may have to come down in price in order to generate new interest in the property. There are companies now that will take your property listing and not provide any service–with the exception of placing the property in the local MLS. Agents working with buyers are not offered a cooperative fee split, or if they are, it's a nominal fee that can be as low as $1.00. So the agent is instructed to bring their buyer's offer direct to the seller and to negotiate directly.

That buyer's agent then, in order to get paid for their work, must write a commission into the contract or will have to collect it directly from their buyer. And if that agent doubts their ability to get paid if they sell a property, what do you think are the prospects of them actually showing it?

This following point is made by our good friend and Realtor®, Mollie Wasserman, from her forthcoming book on Real Estate Consulting:

> "MLS Entry Only" is one of the biggest travesties foisted on the public. Not only is it a legal liability (people think that if you are their agent, you're representing them, no matter what they sign), it doesn't work! That is the big reason I will not offer MLS Entry Only. Despite advertising claims to the contrary, we know from sales data over the last couple of years that MLS Entry Only is usually a waste of money for the vast majority of sellers. The MLS was designed as a co-operative between licensed agents, not an advertising medium for unrepresented sellers. When the MLS is used as intended, agents know that they will have a licensed partner on the other side who will not only provide the fiduciary counsel to their own client, but also complete the many tasks required of an agent. MLS Entry Only listings notoriously get far fewer showings because buyer agents know they will have to deal directly with the seller and often have to do the work for both sides. Because of this, and the lack of fiduciary counsel, many MLS Entry Only listings do not sell, forcing the seller to then hire a full service agent and forfeit their MLS Entry Only fee. If their home does sell, it usually receives thousands of dollars less than it should have for being a party to this consumer rip-off.

Now, consider if you were the buyer and had to pay your agent's commission on top of paying for the home. You could not include the commission in the financing, because it is not in the purchase price. So, it would be additional money out of pocket.

If financing were to be part of the deal, you would likely lose that buyer. And if you will be paying the buyer's agent directly (usually more than half a "normal" listing commission), you might as well engage a full service Realtor® from the beginning, eliminate the headaches and have someone capable, willing, and obligated to provide you with good advice throughout the listing/sale process.

As of this writing, ten states have passed legislation requiring licensed real estate agents to provide a set minimum amount of service, regardless of what they charge. And a number of additional states are considering similar legislation. Part of the impetus has been complaints from homeowners who did not understand that they would have to do virtually everything in the transaction and pay the fees as well. The Department of Justice has indicated that it may take this to court on anti-trust grounds, but the National Association of REALTORS® has said it will aggressively fight for the states and their consumers.

Bundled Service Companies

A relatively new type of brokerage that offers more payment choices are those entities called "bundled service" companies. These are companies that may provide the entire range of real estate service, but let you choose which you want. You may decide, for example, to hold your own open house and do your own advertising, and hence, pay a smaller fee. Ultimately, you get to decide full-service or less. Just be aware of the differences. Accepting less service may save you money, but it places added burden on you to create a sale.

3. The Role of the Internet

Mollie Wasserman's Real Estate Internet Warning©

Despite advertising claims to the contrary, the Internet is *not* an experienced real estate professional. It cannot consult, counsel, advise, have knowledge of local laws and market conditions, make judgments, "own" the result or, most importantly, understand your individual goals and needs, and care about you as a client. Furthermore, data by itself can be very misleading. To obtain an accurate interpretation of any information you're receiving online, please contact a Realtor®.

—Mollie Wasserman, Medway, Massachussets

Given the revolution in technology that we've experienced over the last few years we must look at *what technology can and cannot do*. This differentiation is especially crucial when dealing with real estate, an environment where online companies clutter the bandwidth and your inbox with schemes to save incredible amounts of money and time by using their services.

Now let's be clear: Technology, and specifically the Internet, is a wonderful thing! Technology is a fabulous way to gather data and can do *functionary* tasks better, faster, and cheaper than any human being ever could. But the danger does not lie in understanding that technology. The danger is that by itself, the Internet can never provide the *fiduciary* counsel required in services such as mortgage lending, law, and real estate.

Functionary, fiduciary—why do we keep using these "f" words? Simply, it's very important to understand the difference between the data that you can get online and the advice, counsel, and interpretation of that data that only your Realtor® can provide if you're to get the best deal when you sell a home.

Information Versus Knowledge

As Internet-savvy Realtors® who generate a significant portion of our business online, we are big believers in the free flow of information. You will find that both online and off, this new breed of Realtor® usually provides the most complete sources of information that you'll find anywhere.

Yet, we have had many of our colleagues question why we give out so much information, often saying: "If you give out too much information, people will have no reason to call you." We disagree. Although we give out information freely, we have never had a shortage of requests to retain our services. That's because there's a big difference between *information* and *knowledge.*

John Tuccillo states in his book, *The Eight New Rules of Real Estate,* "Information is a collection of facts or observations about reality. Knowledge is actionable." In today's information age, consumers can increasingly get all the information that they want or need, but it's useless unless someone with expertise in the field can provide the knowledge to allow them to correctly act on it. *Information, without the context of a pro who can share the day-to-day knowledge of the industry, is just* data. *If a consumer were to act on it without context, they could very well reach incorrect conclusions and achieve undesirable results.*

Information is like sand on a beach—it's plentiful and anyone can find it. But if you want to build a sandcastle, you may want to consult the Sandmaster who lives on the beach, who can tell you how much water to use, what weather conditions are best for building, and most importantly, when the tide comes in and how far up. Without this knowledge, you could spend an entire afternoon building a great sandcastle, only to have it washed away!

Myths Involving Real Estate and the Internet

People love to surf the Internet when it comes to real estate. It's estimated that last year, between 70 and 80 percent of homebuyers started their search online. But there are definitely myths about what the Internet can and cannot do. The following myth is one of our favorites:

"The Internet is great! I can . . .

- buy a book
- buy an airline ticket
- buy or sell a house
- get legal advice
- receive a medical opinion

. . . *all* online!"

At what point did the above statement step over the line from fact to myth? If you say after number two, the airline ticket, give yourself a gold star! What's the difference between the first two products and the last three services? Simple. *The first two are commodities bought mostly by price, the last three are services that require counsel, advice, knowledge, and understanding of your individual needs.* The first two are functionary products, the last three are fiduciary services. You can purchase the first two products entirely online and probably save money in the process.

In regards to the last three services, the Internet is a great place to start your search for service providers. But if you try to "go it alone" with just the data you find online, you will very likely risk losing your shirt if you don't consult a local provider who understands your individual needs and is accountable for their services.

Let's look at a couple of obvious examples before turning to real estate. Let's say there's an online site called WeKnowLaw.com. For $39.95, payable in advance by credit card, you can receive a "legal opinion." Does this opinion come from an attorney, a paralegal or a truck driver? The site *says* it's from an attorney, but how do you know for sure? And what if you take this legal advice and your case turns out badly? How do you get out of the deeper legal dilemma you're now in? Local attorneys who are dependent on referrals for future business have a great incentive to stand behind their advice and counsel. Does whoever at WeKnowLaw out there in Dot-Com Land care if you're unhappy with their opinion? In other words, what happens if something goes wrong?

Then there are the online mortgage companies that advertise everywhere. If you've read the business section of the paper lately, you know that many of these companies are not doing so well. Why is this? Well, there are a couple of reasons. First, much of the mortgage process still has to be done locally, so there's little economy to doing the process online, and more importantly, many consumers are finally catching on that interest rates and financing programs are very vulnerable to the old bait and switch that we mentioned earlier. Do you really think for a moment that the online mortgage company in Anywhere Land is particularly concerned if you're unhappy with their services? Local mortgage lenders derive business from local Realtors® and the community. Therefore, they have to make the situation right because they must be *accountable*! The national dot-com isn't.

Now, as we said earlier, the Internet is a wonderful place to shop rates and programs and to educate yourself on the mortgage process. But afterwards, do yourself a favor and bring the best package to your Realtor's® recommended lender and ask if they can match it. Either they will, or they'll tell you why they can't.

Have you ever been to a medical website? There are many wonderful sites out there. If you were to go to one to become a more educated patient, and then take your questions and concerns to your doctor, that would be a very smart use of the Internet. If, however, you were to go to a site and attempt to diagnose yourself, that would be a very unintelligent use of information, with potentially disastrous results.

Real estate is an interesting field in that it combines functionary tasks with fiduciary counsel. Functionary tasks such as property searches or accessing home sales data can always be done cheaper, faster, and better by technology. If that was the whole of real estate, we'd be the first to applaud the national dot-coms popping up online promising to provide you these services without your having to leave the computer. But the problem is, these companies don't tell you what you *don't* get. As an example, there are a couple of companies that heavily advertise that you can get a *free* home valuation online. All you have to do is give them a street address and it's yours. So what *do* you get? (Drum roll please.) A list of homes sold within a one-mile radius of that address. Does this "home valuation," coming from a national site, take into account the power plant going in two blocks away from this home which will affect its value? Has it seen the inside of the home to find out how it compares with others? Does it take into account the railroad tracks on the next street? What about the local economy and the fact that young professionals are moving into the area, accelerating the increase in prices? What about sewer abatements or the newest regulations? A national dot-com can't advise you of any of those things, which could greatly affect the value of the property; but a Realtor® who's working in your interest can.

Please remember that while the Internet can provide information, it cannot interpret it! A Realtor®'s real value is not just in using technology to market your home, but bringing those buyers to you and helping you make the most money when selling your home!

4. How Much Is Your Home Really Worth?

We were thrilled with the way you handled the sale of our home. As residents in our community since 1984, we wanted someone that knew the area and could sell the lifestyle of this community as well as our house. We wanted to get top dollar for it and we didn't want the process to drag on indefinitely.

You not only under-promised what you could do for us, you over-delivered by selling our house for the price we wanted and in a record amount of time. We can't thank you enough for all you did and would, without hesitation, refer you to anyone considering buying or selling their home.

—M. Gordon Stevens, Burke, Virginia

When you are ready to sell your home, you must determine the "asking" price with your Realtor®'s advice. This should be a compromise between the fair market value and the price that you hope to get. Once you determine this number, you should also adjust it to make sure that you leave room to negotiate with prospective buyers. Although this sounds like we are telling you to expect to negotiate down the sales price, you should know that in some markets you may get the opportunity to negotiate up! So unlike many other purchases in this country, real estate prices should always be negotiable.

Here is another reason to hire a Realtor®. A good, experienced Realtor® in your area will often know just by looking at your home what it can expect to sell for in the current market. Not only might they know the sale prices of similar homes that have sold in the neighborhood, but your Realtor® may know the homes' original listing prices and how much sellers in your neighborhood have been willing to negotiate.

Whether or not you decide to use a Realtor®, there are two predominant ways to determine a home's value: an appraisal and a competitive market analysis (CMA). What you should expect to learn through either process is the approximate value of your home. The reality is that until your home actually sells, there is no precise way to determine exactly what your home is worth. In the business, we say that your home is worth exactly what someone is willing to pay for it. An appraiser will tell you that a home's value is equal to an amount agreed to between an able and willing buyer and an able and willing seller, when neither person is unduly influenced by outside forces.

Home Appraisal

Although an appraisal is usually ordered by the buyer's lender to satisfy lending requirements, it can also be a worthwhile investment for a seller. Appraisals are commonly seen as the best way to determine your home's most precise value. In Virginia, a home appraisal should only be done by a licensed appraiser, and your Realtor® can usually provide a referral to a competent one. The appraiser reviews various factors to determine the approximate sale price of your home. These factors include looking at historical records of the property and the area, looking at the property's prior sales performance, and reviewing the current condition of the property. For more detailed information on how appraisals work, contact the Appraisal Institute at 875 Michigan Ave., Suite 2400, Chicago, IL 60611, or www.appraisalinstitute.org.

There are also ways in which you, as the homeowner, can ensure that the appraisal looks out for your best interests. First, you should make sure that your house is in the best possible condition (see more on this in Chapter 6). You should also make sure that the appraiser is both licensed and qualified. Some states have few or no requirements regarding who can appraise homes; therefore, there are some appraisers who will incorrectly value your home due to inexperience. Don't be afraid to ask the appraiser how long they have been working in the profession and how many homes they have appraised in your area in the last few months.

Market Value

The most common method used by Realtors® to determine the sales price of your home is a competitive market analysis (CMA). A CMA is an estimated value of your home, based on the sales price and similar attributes of other properties in the area. CMA's may be less precise than appraisals, but they are generally a reliable method for determining the asking price of your home.

While less reliable than a local Realtor® who is familiar with your market, another source for obtaining a CMA is the Internet. There are now many on-line companies that will analyze sales information of residential properties, and for a nominal charge will value your home based on sales prices in your area. However, you should also be aware that online CMAs only search public geographical records to determine a home's value, so they can not take into consideration the condition or precise location of a home. Although these services are not yet available in all areas, it certainly seems to be the new trend in roughly determining home values.

It will also help if, with your Realtor®, you look at other comparable homes currently on the market in your area and compare their similarities and differences. This will help you decide the list price of your home, and help you see exactly who you may be competing against for that perfect buyer.

We will generally recommend a range. You can start in the high end of that range if you are not in a hurry to sell, and you are more interested in maximizing your profit, or net return. You would list in the low end of that range if your goal is to sell quickly. Remember that regardless of what list price you choose, the actual sales price may be slightly higher or lower. But if for some reason your house is not selling, you and your Realtor® should consider lowering the price. Beware of having your mind set on some magic number given by a CMA. Remember that these are only approximations of the real value of your home. The economy, and the market, can actually change in relatively short periods of time. In addition, no matter how you try to determine a price, your home may have unique features that are just not present in any other home.

5. Selling Your Home in an Up or Down Market

I want to thank you for the wonderful job you did in selling my condo. I was pleased to have the offer less than two weeks after listing and it was such a relief to close the sale in less than two months from start to finish. Your efforts made the quick sale possible. You helped me set a fair asking price and made excellent suggestions on how to improve the appearance of my property. You staged the property so that it truly looked like a model home, even though it was vacant. Your brochure was beautiful with the photos and floor plan that would help a buyer remember my unit, and made it stand out from all the competing properties on the market.

You handled all the problems—big and small—that cropped up, particularly in taking care of the home inspection items that came up as well as the termite inspection. I didn't have to worry about a thing or take time off from work to find workmen and arrange for the work to be done.

It was a pleasure to have you represent me and if I ever need to buy or sell real estate, I'll look forward to working with you again.

—Marry Gallagher, Arlington, Virginia

Although the asking price may need slight modifications, regardless of the real estate market, a good Realtor® will be able to help you sell your home. This may be important to the many sellers out there who cannot wait for a market turnaround. The reality is, if the house is priced fairly and your house is in a condition that appeals to the average buyer, you should be able to sell your home regardless of the market.

Besides the "asking" price, there are many things that can affect how quickly you sell your home, but we will start with price.

Price

For obvious reasons, the asking price is the most important factor in determining how fast your home sells. Despite the desire to make sure that you price your home high enough to make a profit, as well as leaving negotiating room, you should be aware that overpricing your home is the most common and dangerous mistake that you can make as a seller, and is more dangerous in a buyer's market than a seller's market.

A home may be overpriced for many reasons. Some sellers consider their first asking price to be a "trial balloon," where they just want to see if they can attract a better-than-normal offer. Others simply insist that their home is worth more than any objective market analysis would indicate. For example, sellers who have been trying to sell their house themselves for months may now want to raise the price since they are paying a Realtor® for representation; the sellers still want their net price, so they try to add sales commissions to the listed price. Homes like this usually stay on the market the longest and end up being sold for less than market value. One of the primary reasons so many FSBOs fail is because the seller is personally biased. It is easy to convince yourself that something you own is worth more than its real value. It's also why so many Realtors®, when selling their home, actually list with other Realtors®, or at least rely on the advice of others. Objectivity is paramount.

Many sellers know of a home that sold for a high price in their neighborhood, and want to know why their home should not be similarly priced. But they may be unfamiliar with the particular differences between that house and their own that would justify the difference in value.

The bottom line is, don't overprice your home. Professionals know that the longer a house stays on the market, the lower the selling price will be in comparison to the original asking price. More often than not, your first offer will be your best. So if you overprice your home by 5 percent, you could end up losing 10 percent or more, and wait months to sell your home.

This leaves us with the question of how to modify the price of your home, in either an up or down market, to avoid overpricing. This is where a Realtor®'s advice can be invaluable. Unlike a typical seller, who is only familiar with the markets that effect either the sale or purchase of their own homes, an experienced Realtor® will have the knowledge of many years of market changes and fluctuations. They will also have a database of important sales statistics which they can use to expand their knowledge base. This can turn a guessing game into an educated pricing decision.

Depending on the circumstances, you may also want to consider underpricing your home. This option can be appealing when you need to sell fast, possibly because you are moving out of the area for work or to close on a replacement property. In the recent past, Susan has sold several properties where the buyer was the first and only party to see the property. These were cases where the buyers had difficulty finding the right property, the new listings were underpriced, and they fit the buyer's needs perfectly. Even with full-priced offers, they got bargains. Good Realtors® check for new listings every day, and when a good deal comes up, they call the buyer immediately to see the property. Underpricing can sell homes *quickly*!

It is also important to know that there are buyers in every price range in your market just waiting for the next property listing. They've already seen everything that fits their criteria without finding the "right" home. If yours is priced right, and it fits, you could have a quick sale. However, if it is overpriced, the buyer may not see your home at all or won't make an offer. Overpricing can cause you to lose that buyer forever.

If for some reason your house has been on the market for longer than the normal range in your market, action besides just lowering the price can and should be taken. If no one has even looked at your home, you can be relatively sure that price is the issue. Somehow, despite you and your Realtor®'s best efforts, your home is not adequately priced for your area. It may be because of a severe "buyer's market," or it may be because others in your area have taken less than full value for their homes for one reason or another. If this is the case, making adjustments to your asking price will be necessary if you are unwilling to wait to sell your home.

If you have had people looking at your home, but you still have not had any reasonable offers, you should find out what specifically is discouraging buyers. There are several ways to do so. First, your Realtor® should be getting feedback from both the buyers who saw your home and from the Realtors® who showed it. Not all Realtors® will respond, but the feedback can be invaluable.

A word of caution. It is easy to get defensive when buyer feedback indicates "the home is overpriced" or "the floor plan doesn't work." We have had sellers say, "Well, if they don't like the price, tell them to make an offer and we'll see what we can do." The fact is that most buyers, while willing to make an offer under the asking price, do not feel comfortable "lowballing" an offer. They simply feel that negotiation would be futile.

A good Realtor® will seek brute honesty in feedback and will convey that to you undiluted. And while an occasional buyer may respond too personally (e.g., "what a horrid floor plan"), it's important to look at all the feedback with your Realtor® to determine the next steps to take.

If your home has languished on the market for several months, it may be a good time to take another look at your competition. Your Realtor® can set showings for you on competing properties, and this could serve as a reliable reality check.

Negotiating Tools

In general terms, there are two primary approaches to negotiating a deal when price alone is the major consideration. One is to start low and know you will probably reach an agreed-upon price somewhere close to the asking price. In fact, one of the jobs of your Realtor® is to try to determine your bottom line. The second approach is to make a "take it or leave it" offer. If you only want to sell at the price that you and your Realtor® have determined is fair, then this is a realistic approach to take. Then buyers will only be able to negotiate on "cosmetic" items like the closing date or what is included in the sale. Believe it or not, we had a number of deals accepted on that basis, but usually when the house was listed for slightly under the market value.

The vast majority of real estate deals, when both sides are represented, should come down to what is fair. It should end up being a win/win situation, where everyone feels satisfied with the deal. We have all dealt with buyers who "want a deal" and who are unwilling to pay fair market value for any property. They want to steal it, to stick a knife in the seller's back, and then twist it. They are only looking for someone who is vulnerable and has to sell at any price. We usually send away this kind of buyer.

Now, it is true some deals are made this way. We have found properties that must be sold quickly to avoid bankruptcy, or that are on the verge of foreclosure. We have not hesitated to get one of our buyers into such a deal. But your Realtor® is there to protect you from buyers who take the attitude that you can only be happy if you have "screwed" the seller. This attitude is really just corruptive of the whole process of real estate sales.

So, if you haven't already, you and your Realtor® should now prepare for negotiation by formulating a game plan. You should both be clear about what is vital to the deal and what you can give up. Most bottom lines should include some unnecessary items you can give up without feeling deprived, while giving the buyers the sense they won some concessions. It is also important to understand that there are many more things to negotiate besides price. In fact, there are occasions when price, although important in reeling a buyer in, is the *least* important negotiating objective.

For example, you may need a really quick close—you will lose a home you are trying to purchase and you need the sale proceeds immediately. If the buyers are renters, you may not have a problem; but if they also have a house they need to sell, it may mean convincing them to own two homes for a period of time, and you may have to concede to the offering price in order to get what you need. On the other hand, you may have just put in a brand-new lighting fixture that you would love to keep, but if it means getting your asking price, it may be worth parting with. In fact, we always recommend that you remove any items that you definitely want to keep before putting your house on the market, so that you don't have to say "no" and potentially waste negotiating power on trivial items. The bottom line is that it is important to know, and to clearly communicate to your agent, those things that are important to you and those that are not.

Always try to negotiate from a position of strength. You can contribute to a stronger negotiating position by not overpricing your home. It will also help if you have taken the steps described in the next chapter to make your home as attractive as possible. And, if you are looking to buy another home, it will be to your advantage to wait until you are under contract with a buyer before you make an offer of your own.

Your Realtor® will also try to find out what might motivate the buyers. While it is not always possible to determine their motivations up front, it is usually worth trying. For example, if you find out that the buyers are moving from out of state and need extra moving time, you can give them the time they need in exchange for taking something like the washer and dryer. If you are not in a hurry to move, and you can make a closing date or possession date agreeable to the buyers, don't you think they might be willing to negotiate on price?

If you find out that the buyers are being transferred and need to move quickly, or are getting divorced, or are facing a termination of their rental lease, you will have accumulated information that is important to your negotiating process. Once you know as much as you can about the buyers' position, and you and your Realtor® have a clear picture of your negotiating position, you are one step closer to selling your home.

Another useful strategy to sell your home is giving the buyer a break. If negotiations are stalled, you might offer to throw in the riding lawn mower, or offer to clean the carpets after you have vacated. Small gestures can be very valuable. If a buyer is on the fence, a seller who appears willing to do something extra may have the right stuff to seal a deal. And at the end of the day, that $500 riding lawn mower may have saved you an extra month's wait in selling your home. Occasionally even offering a home warranty can do the trick.

Condition

You may not have control over the real estate market or your neighborhood's sales prices, but there is one area where you can personally make a huge impact: the condition of your home. Although this will be discussed in much more detail in the following chapter, making sure that your home is in the best possible condition will greatly enhance your odds of selling your home quickly and at a good price.

Susan works with a Realtor® known in the real estate industry as "Lox and Bagel." The nickname comes from the fact that he often "dresses" his listings for open houses, including setting the kitchen table with a lovely brunch including *synthetic* bagels topped with lox! Realtors® call this "staging" a home.

As silly as this sounds, his houses sell, and not just because of the synthetic food. On Sunday mornings, when most of his open houses are held, he provides his guests with an idea of what it would be like to wake up and have a beautiful brunch in this very home, which he hopes will soon be theirs. He even draws baths, complete with candles, champagne and strawberries. The bottom line is that when you view his homes, you know exactly how wonderful it could be to live there. Just as in magazine or television advertising, subtleties can make a huge difference.

It is important to realize that when a potential buyer views your home, you have your one and only chance to make the right impression. You may know that the dishes are usually washed and the lawn raked, but a potential homeowner only knows what they see on that first viewing. So before you cost yourself time and money, make sure your house is "dressed and ready" for sale!

6. Dressed and Ready for Sale

I came to the United States from Trinidad in 1993. My brother, Michael, introduced me to Susan, who had recently helped him and his wife, Beverly, purchase their first home. After talking with her and her lender, I realized I wasn't quite ready to purchase a home here in America. I have a strong faith. Susan was great and never tried to discourage me. Instead, she stayed in contact. It took a few years to get started, but in the last five years, Susan, coupled with my strong belief in God, has helped me purchase three homes and sell two. I now own my own single family home in Fairfax County on a quarter acre lot backing to parkland. The American Dream of home ownership is a reality for me. Praise Jesus.

—Marlene George, Springfield, Virginia

Buying a home can be one of the most emotional purchases a person or family makes. A buyer may see that perfect bay window with the window seat they've always dreamed of and know that your home has to be theirs. So in order to have the most successful experience in selling your home, you must appeal to the *emotions* of potential buyers.

The reality is that what your home looks like matters, a lot! Deep down most buyers want a perfect new house, regardless of what they can really afford. That's why builders spend thousands of dollars decorating model homes. No matter the age of your house, your job is to make it appear as new as possible without wasting money. Obviously, if your house was perfect you probably wouldn't want to move, but the point is to make it as appealing as possible.

We always recommend to our sellers that a good place to start is with a thorough inspection. Take a pad and paper and walk from room to room, writing down what you see. Don't just focus on problem areas, look for what you should highlight. Are there wonderful French doors hidden by worn curtains? Is the fireplace blocked from view by too much old furniture? You should not only tour every room, but inspect the entire property. Look at the house through the eyes of a buyer as if you were going to make an offer. What would you want to see? Maybe even enlist the help of an honest and impartial friend or family member to help you be more objective. If a buyer has a choice between two comparable properties that are similarly priced, they will choose the one in the best condition.

Dos and Don'ts

There are some very simple and inexpensive things that you can do, or that you should avoid, when you are selling your home. By following these simple tips, you can not only increase the sale price of your home, but hopefully ensure a quick sale. Remember you have a very valuable item to sell. So like a sophisticated salesperson, you should make sure that the product you are offering is useful and appealing.

Tip 1: Get rid of any and all clutter. Piles of books and magazines, and bags of recycling can be such a negative distraction that potential buyers might walk right out before passing the entry hall. The goal is to make your house spotless. The less clutter there is, the more open and spacious your home will appear. Too much furniture and knick-knacks always make a room look smaller than it is. And don't forget the closets and the garage. Storage space is an important concern of many buyers, so the less cluttered these spaces are, the more space buyers think they are getting. Don't wait until you pack to throw out those unneeded items—now is the time to do it. These things cost nothing more than time, but in the scope of a sale can be invaluable. There's no need to make major changes, as most homeowners want to decorate themselves. You want to give buyers a spacious and clean blank canvas. Consider renting a storage space. The cost is minimal and the payback immense.

Tip 2: Avoid air fresheners. To prospective buyers, air fresheners seem like cover ups. You are better off making sure that your home has been well aired out, particularly if you are a smoker. Try using strategic fresh flowers to add a touch of ambience as well as a fresh scent, or bake fresh cookies or bread. Susan suggests renting an air purifier. These units actually eliminate, not mask, animal and smoke odors. There are many on the market so ask your Realtor® for recommendations as oftentimes they will have access to such a unit and can offer it to you at a minimal cost.

Tip 3: Make sure that your home is as inviting as possible. This means turning off the television and any other distracting electronic devices. Instead, try using soft classical or jazz music to set the tone. You also want inviting lighting. Make sure you have high-watt bulbs in dark rooms and soft lighting in areas where you want to detract attention. Regardless, make sure all light bulbs are working.

Tip 4: Another important suggestion is to make sure that pets and children are not around when your house is being shown to prospective buyers. It is best to assume that buyers don't have pets or children and let them ask questions about how a home can accommodate their needs if necessary. The bottom line is that if a buyer is allergic to cats or dogs, your beloved pet may drive them out before giving your home a chance.

Tip 5: You should avoid potentially offensive and/or embarrassing items. Given the vast majority of cultures that we deal with here in Northern Virginia, what may be pleasant to one may be totally offensive to another. It really comes down to a judgment call between you and your Realtor®. The safest bet: if in doubt—eliminate!

Tip 6: If you have furniture that is old or showing its wear, it may be worthwhile to remove it (either by storing or donating it) before showing your home. Unattractive furnishings can distract potential buyers. It is usually better to have more open space than to fill it with marginal items.

Tip 7: If you have wood floors in good condition you should be sure to show them off. Conversely, cover any old or worn floors with clean and tidy rugs. Additionally, if you have carpeting, make sure that you have it properly cleaned. In fact, stained or dirty carpet is such a huge turnoff to buyers, that depending on the condition, it may be worthwhile to replace it with inexpensive neutral carpeting.

Tip 8: A little-known secret of the trade is to make sure that you don't leave your car in the driveway. When a buyer pulls up they should see the home, not your cars. Let them feel like the driveway is theirs, and maybe even visualize themselves coming home. If you can't park your car in the garage because of clutter, reread Tip 1.

Tip 9: You should also make sure that any important papers, prescription drugs and valuables are put away in a safe place. The reality is that buyers are strangers that you are letting into your home. Although a Realtor® will always be there to show your home, it is best not to take chances with your private and valuable items.

Tip 10: Clean sells. Be anal about it. Scrub down bathrooms, wash windows, dust ceiling fans, check corners for cobwebs, and vacuum air vents. Pretend you are the buyer and look at your home through a buyer's eyes. If you don't have the time, consider hiring a cleaning company and, if necessary, employ them on a weekly basis while your house is on the market.

Tip 11: Virginia is a *caveat emptor* state, meaning buyer beware. In other words, it is up to the buyer to make sure the condition of the house they are considering is acceptable to them. Spending a few hundred dollars on pre-listing repairs could end up netting you twice that in a final sales price. Remember that per sales contract, the seller warrants the following to be in normal working order by possession date, unless agreed upon otherwise: existing appliances, heating, cooling, plumbing, electrical, mechanical systems and equipment, smoke and heat detectors (as required by county code).

Tip 12: Connected to Tip 9 is the rule that you should always have an agent present when you are showing your home. This is not only a safety issue, but how else can you ensure that prospective buyers have all the information they need to make an offer on your home? Buyers are savvy; they expect their questions to be answered by a knowledgeable representative.

Making the Buyer Comfortable

Potential buyers may be entering their future home, and can't help but emotionally connect with the surroundings. You can take advantage of this. You can make coffee or bake cookies. This is not only a kind gesture, but adds pleasing, comfortable aromas.

Another useful tool is to give a list of your favorite features to your agent. This way your Realtor® can draw buyers to the best parts of your home. What made you want to buy your home is likely a selling point for prospective buyers. The more your Realtor® points out to potential buyers, the more comfortable they will feel, and the less time they will need to spend learning about the home for themselves.

One area over which you may have little control is your neighborhood. Regardless, we all know how important a factor this is in buying a home. But don't fret; there are some small things that you can do that can make a big difference. You can help clean up graffiti in the neighborhood; you can clean up garbage in the street; you can have the city tow away inoperative or abandoned cars. In the larger scheme, you can team up with neighbors to form a neighborhood cleanup group or a Neighborhood Watch program. Prospective buyers may be relieved to know that even though you are leaving, they are moving into a neighborhood that cares.

Another thing that most buyers are looking for is a relatively modern home. As we discussed earlier, buyers want a home to appear new. Things that substantially date your house, like popcorn ceilings, metal banisters, and wood paneling, can make a sale more difficult. It's worthwhile to look into the cost of replacing, painting or removing these items. It may very well be a great investment.

Today's homebuyer is looking for "character." Just as popcorn ceilings are out, molding and natural woods are in. Adding molding can be a relatively inexpensive do-it-yourself project with substantial returns.

If you are going to spend money on your home, there are two places where your investment will have the greatest payback: the kitchen and the bathroom. Replacing kitchen counters with granite and floors with wood or ceramic tile alone can brighten up a dated kitchen. Likewise, bathroom remodels can be moderately priced and can substantially update your home. You don't need to take any of these steps to sell your home, but be aware of what buyers will be looking for, and how you can best meet their needs. Just making your home sparkling clean can make a huge difference. Sellers must consider these factors and decide for themselves how much time and money they can invest in the final sale price of their home.

Exterior

First impressions, better known as "curb appeal," are extremely important, and the first thing that prospective buyers will see is the outside of your home. The exterior not only speaks for itself, but it tells potential buyers what they can expect to find inside. The reality is that if the exterior of your home is in a bad state, many buyers will just keep on driving. If you drove up to a house with peeling paint, dead plants, and falling rain gutters, you wouldn't expect the inside to be taken care of, would you? For some small things you can do to make sure that the outside of your home is as well-dressed as the inside, see our checklist at the end of the chapter.

Amenities

The most common problem we see after a closing is that the seller takes an item from the property that the buyer assumed was part of the sale. This goes back to an important point that we discussed earlier: Make sure that items you want to keep are removed from the house before you show it to prospective buyers. The bottom line is that there are some items that will automatically become part of the property once title is passed to the buyer, regardless of whether you assumed it was yours to keep. This is referred to as the *law of fixtures.*

The law of fixtures basically says that fixtures are part of the property and cannot be removed. Fixtures are anything that is permanently attached to the property by attachments such as bolts or screws. Some items are easy to understand as fixtures, such as counters, sinks, or flooring. But some areas are more complicated. For example, a built-in dishwasher is a fixture, since it can't just be unplugged and removed, but a refrigerator is too, even though it can be unplugged and removed. In Northern Virginia it is customary that it remains with the house. Similarly, window treatments are only considered fixtures if they are screwed or bolted in. So you can take curtains, but not the rod if it is bolted to the wall.

Another common area of confusion is lighting. If light fixtures are bolted to the wall or ceiling, they are part of the sale, even including expensive chandeliers and antiques, because if you show them, they become part of the transaction. The only way to avoid this problem is by removing these items (and replacing them with inexpensive fixtures) before showing your home or in the listing agreement, note them as not part of the sale. Unlike nonfixtures (refrigerators, washers and dryers), a buyer does not even have to request these items in the contract.

One last item to consider: bathroom mirrors. Several times, Susan has been on the buying-end when a very fancy bathroom mirror, on the wall at the time of contract, disappeared before the walk-through. In one instance, it was a treasured antique and the seller had no intention of conveying it with the sale of the house. No mention was ever made during contract negotiations that the mirror would be removed or replaced. Mirrors appear to fall into a gray area. Oftentimes, they are fixed to a wall and fall under the law of fixtures. In this case, it was considered a wall hanging and in the eyes of the seller, a nonfixture. Moral of the story: replace any prized bathroom mirrors with ones that will convey with the property.

Real Problems

There may be some real problems with your house that need to be repaired before you sell it. Except in a tight market, major "as-is" fixer-uppers are hard to sell.

In fact, you should never spend money on cosmetic repairs unless you know that your home is structurally sound. If there are genuine problems with your home, you should either spend the money to address them, or understand that you will have to sell it as a fixer-upper for a reduced price.

A few years ago, one of Susan's clients, Tim, listed a rather old Cape Cod–style home that had been in his family for generations. He had recently inherited the home and wasn't particularly interested in fixing it up or living in it, so he decided to put it on the market. He informed his original Realtor®, whom we'll call Joe, that he didn't know much about the condition of the house, but that he did remember that the bathroom on the second floor had flooded a few years before, leaking through the roof and eventually damaging two of the downstairs bedrooms. Because the carpet had been replaced and the walls repainted, there was no visible sign of the incident.

Joe advised Tim not to say anything to avoid scaring away potential buyers. Taking Joe's advice, he accepted a full-price offer and never made any mention of the water damage.

During the inspection, the water damage was discovered and the buyers not only backed out, but they threatened both Tim and Joe with lawsuits for failing to disclose known damage to the property.

As it turned out, Tim came to Susan's office. She not only helped Tim with the mess that Joe had created, but she put his family home back on the market with full disclosure of the water damage, and listed it for only $10,000 less than the original asking price. Although it took a few months to sell, she finally sold the home to a handyman and his wife, because they knew that they could make the necessary repairs for under $3,000 and were happy to have saved some money! There is always a buyer for every home; the important thing is finding the *right* buyer.

If you suspect that your home has serious issues such as structural damage, termites, mold, sink-holes, lead paint, radon, flood damage or a wet basement, you should start with your own home inspection. A visual inspection will help you pinpoint potentially serious issues so that you can have them assessed by a specialist.

You should also be aware that once you know about defects, you are legally obligated to disclose them to potential buyers. You and your agent must disclose any *known* material defects in your property. Although if you are selling your house "as is" the buyer must accept any conditions as part of the sale, they still must be fully disclosed.

Checklist

Begin with the Exterior

1. If your house doesn't look good from the outside, a potential buyer may decide not to go inside. Make sure the lawn is well manicured. Be sure to fertilize to make it look lush and green. A well-manicured lawn, neatly trimmed shrubs, and cleanly swept sidewalks create a good first impression.

2. Mulch flower beds and, depending on the season, add color with plantings. Two pots of flowers and a fresh welcome mat can draw the buyer into the house.

3. Trim or cut back overgrown shrubs. Clean gutters—little saplings growing out of a gutter can give the impression of poor maintenance there and throughout the house.

4. Paint the house if necessary. (If you do decide to paint your house, drive through new neighborhoods and choose a contemporary, neutral color. Don't paint your house the same old color it was in 1970.)
5. Clean stains and oil from sidewalks and driveways. A badly stained driveway suggests that the house may not have been well maintained.
6. Replace cracked or broken windows and torn screens.
7. Hose down the entrance of your house to get rid of annoying cobwebs and dead bugs.
8. Make sure the entry light and doorbell are in good working order.
9. Inspect the roof. Make repairs as necessary.
10. Make sure the front door is easy to open and close. Use silicone spray or graphite in the lock, and if necessary, paint the front door. First impressions are lasting and a new coat of paint suggests a well-cared-for home.
11. Put a fresh coat of paint on your mailbox.
12. Be sure driveways and sidewalks are free of ice and snow in the winter.

Now Let's Look at the Interior

1. Begin with a full housecleaning from top to bottom. Clean out closets and throw away unused items. Make sure that clothes are hung neatly and shoes are tidily arranged.

Eliminating clutter makes your home look more spacious.

2. Make sure the walls are clean and free of smudges and fingerprints. Give them a fresh coat of paint if washing doesn't do the trick. There are a myriad of new products that remove scrapes and smudges from walls. Oftentimes this eliminates the need for a painting.
3. Arrange furniture to make your rooms appear more spacious. Get rid of badly worn furniture or place it in storage.
4. Wash the windows, including the sills, inside and out!
5. Wash, replace or just eliminate the curtains.
6. Clean the carpets and wax the floors. If you have ceramic tile floors, consider bleaching the grout.
7. Repair any sticking doors.
8. Fix leaky faucets and clean the water stains from the sinks, toilets and shower doors.
9. Replace burned-out light bulbs and make sure that all light fixtures are in good working order.
10. The kitchen is the most important room in your house. Make it bright and inviting. Wash the walls and cabinets or give them a new coat of paint if necessary. Clean the vent hood. If the floor is badly worn, consider replacing it.

11. Make the bathrooms sparkle! Repair or replace old caulk in showers and tubs. Place fresh towels in the bathrooms.
12. Clean the bedrooms and replace faded curtains and bedspreads.
13. Clean the basement and the garage. Get rid of items you no longer use or put them in storage. Make sure there is plenty of light in the basement.
14. If the basement is dark and gloomy, consider giving the walls and floor a coat of white paint.
15. Make sure your house smells fresh and clean. Nothing is a bigger turnoff to a buyer than a smelly dog bed or dirty litter box.
16. If there is a fireplace, have the chimney cleaned. Soot has an odor!
17. Have the HVAC system cleaned, inspected and replace the filter (home inspectors love to make this an issue).

7. Screening Prospective Buyers

We had grown tired of being landlords and we wanted to purchase a single family home. To do that, we needed to sell our investment condo first and then concentrate on selling our townhouse while at the same time finding our new home. There was a lot of co-ordination involved, especially since we were selling and buying in a strong seller's market. Both properties sold quickly. Finding a new house, however, was a little tougher. Susan was able to negotiate a strong kick-out clause in the sale of our townhouse that enabled us to cancel the sales contract within a 60-day period if we were unable to find the right home for our family. Fortunately we didn't have to use that clause. Susan kept on top of things and we're so glad she did because a few hours could have lost us the house we wanted and ultimately got.

—Mary Beth and Michael Groarke,
Reston, Virginia

Motivation

The motivation for selling your home will be a substantial factor in determining the kind of buyer you are looking for. For example, if you need to sell your home because you have been offered a job in a new state, you may be willing to look for a broader range of buyers than if you are merely selling in order to buy a bigger home. Likewise, a buyer looking for an investment property may want different things than one who is looking for a home for their family. Knowing both your motivation and the motivation of your prospective buyers can help the negotiating process. There are many types of buyers with many different financial backgrounds, and sometimes a buyer with a no-money-down loan program can be just as good as an all-cash buyer.

Conventional Financing

When selling your home, you will likely be familiar with some of the basics of financing based upon your own experiences as a buyer. However, there are some important aspects of financing about which you should be knowledgeable to ensure that your perfect buyer can actually afford your home. How the buyer intends to pay for your home, and whether or not they are qualified for financing, is really the most important aspect of the entire sales transaction. We all know that without the money, there is no sale.

There are three primary sources for financing the purchase of a home: banks and credit unions, mortgage bankers and mortgage brokers. Most people are aware that banks and credit unions loan money for home purchases, including the former Savings and Loan associations. Savings and Loans, banks, and credit unions lend money directly to the buyer from their own pool of funds, usually based on customer deposits. The individuals that work for the bank are usually called *loan officers*. Loan officers are often paid commission in addition to their salary, which provides their incentive to get loan applications.

Mortgage bankers are also direct lenders and use their own funds, or those of wealthy investors, but they usually do not keep the loan. They will often sell off the loan to a government-sanctioned major home lender like Freddie Mac or Fannie Mae. You might not even know if your loan is sold off, as mortgage bankers often continue to service a loan by mailing statements and collecting payments.

Mortgage brokers shop around for buyers of loans, searching for the lender with the program or interest rate that fits their client's situation. They take the application and can apply to dozens of lenders like banks and mortgage bankers, and act as intermediaries between borrowers and lenders. They can't control interest rates or terms and are usually paid by both the buyer and the lender through closing fees or points. The points paid to buy the loan are often the same as going directly through the lender. One point equals 1 percent of the loan amount. Regardless of whether a buyer uses a broker or a banker, the key is making sure that your buyer has obtained financing prior to making an offer on your home.

Prequalification and Preapproval

The terms prequalification and preapproval are often used by buyers and their agents, and it is extremely important that you know the significant difference between them. The difference is like *thinking* you can afford to buy a home as opposed to having the bank say you qualify. A prequalification letter says the buyer earns enough money to buy a home in a certain price range. Unfortunately, this is based on information given to a bank or mortgage broker by the buyer over the phone. The lender has not verified the buyer's income or run a credit report. Therefore they do not know if the buyer's credit is wonderful or terrible, or if they can secure a loan to fit the buyer's budget.

On the other hand, if a buyer has a preapproval letter, the lender has checked the buyer's credit, gotten basic information on their income and debts, and knows approximately the size of mortgage the buyer will qualify for. Based on the verification, the buyer would be approved for a loan. Obviously, you want to make sure that the buyer is not just prequalified to buy your home, but that they are actually preapproved.

Many lenders also perform "desktop underwriting." If the buyer's credit is good enough, and if it appears their income and debt ratios are strong, the lender can submit a loan application immediately by computer and then receive, almost immediately, an answer from an underwriter. Usually, it will come in the form of full loan approval up to a certain amount, subject to an appraisal of value on the property or with certain conditions that have to be met, such as verification of the information submitted. This is, of course, the best kind of information to receive from a buyer.

When you enter into a contract with a buyer there will likely be a deadline by which they must have full loan approval. If they do not obtain full loan approval by the contract deadline, the buyer may terminate the contract. If the buyer does not terminate the contract, they will be obligated to purchase the home or lose their earnest money deposit. This ensures that your interests are protected.

Creative Financing

Buyers that have trouble getting financing through the normal programs may need to get creative. Some ideas our borrowers like are the *NIV* or *no-doc* loan. With enough money down, usually 20 percent but sometimes only 10 percent, buyers can get one of these loans. NIV stands for "no income verification," and designates a loan where the lender feels secure enough with the size of the down payment that they don't concern themselves with verifying the income stated on the loan application. The lender may simply verify that the buyer is employed and that they actually have the resources necessary to cover the down payment and closing costs. A no-doc loan is a loan where the lender does not require documentation of either income or assets (assets in this case being the money to cover down payment and closing costs). Both of these loans will have a higher interest rate, as much as 1 to 2 percent higher than conforming loans. But when buyers can't secure normal financing, these are still good loans to go after.

Many Realtors® have also identified certain people who have money to invest, and who would like to earn somewhat more than the prevailing 30-year Treasury rate. For 1 or 2 percent above the current 30-year rate, they are often willing to finance a smaller mortgage themselves. Sometimes such loans have balloon payments, meaning that after a period of smaller payments (perhaps five years), the entire amount becomes due. For people who have had credit problems but can demonstrate they are making efforts to clean up their credit, a loan such as this will often get them to the point where they can get conventional refinancing long before a balloon payment becomes due. When a buyer has very little cash to put down, a private lender may take other collateral instead, such as cars or business equipment.

There are many types of creative financing. All of them carry more risk to the buyer than normal conventional financing, and most will cost more in terms of interest rates. But there is really no risk to you as long as the buyer has been preapproved. When you are looking for the right buyer, knowing that they have secured financing, even if through unconventional means, will ensure that your sale will be successful. Sometimes it's the only way to make a deal work, and if so, you shouldn't be afraid to sell to someone who is using creative financing. Just make sure you ask a lot of questions and have your Realtor® at your side.

8. Closing the Deal

I first met Susan when a friend of mine decided to look for a home to buy. I went along on several home visits and came to like Susan. When it was time for me to buy a home, I gravitated to that which was familiar—Susan. To me, Susan was more than just a real estate agent, she was knowledgeable about the area, housing, financing options, and was very willing to help sort through the many options available to me in a market unfamiliar to me. Further, she was professional without being cold or stuffy, personable, easy to talk with, and willing to listen and digest what I wanted and needed.

That was in 1999. Since then I have sold that first home and bought a new single family home all with Susan as my real estate agent. She worked hard to get me a fair price for the home I sold and the home I bought and did this in a market that was aggressive and difficult. I have recommended Susan to others and will continue to recommend her without hesitation to anyone who is in need of an exceptional Realtor®.

—K. Watt Lough, Alexandria, VA

Once a potential buyer has decided that they are interested in purchasing your home, their agent will prepare the actual offer, called a *purchase offer* or a *contract to buy and sell property.* The offer will then be submitted to you and your agent to be evaluated. In some states, the potential buyer may also present you with a deposit, also called *earnest money,* to signify that they are serious about buying the home, that they intend to perform as promised under the offer, and that they will come to closing with the balance of the money needed to close the purchase. Some Realtors® place a great deal of importance on the amount of earnest money presented with the offer and feel the more earnest money presented, the better the buyer.

In Virginia, once everyone makes their changes and signs the offer, it becomes ratified and you and the buyer are either contingent with no kick-out or contingent with a kick-out. A contract is not considered "under contract" until all contingencies have been removed. Contingent with *no* kick-out means the buyer does not have a home to sell as a condition of purchasing your home. Contingent *with* a kick-out means the buyer has a home they must sell before they can proceed with the purchase of your home. The buyer's earnest money is held by whomever is designated in the contract, usually the buyer agent's brokerage firm or the title company, until all of the terms of the offer are met, and the closing is held. The closing then occurs according to the terms of the contract, with buyers, sellers, their agents, and a settlement agent all signing the appropriate closing documents. Additionally, a real estate closing is considered a legal transaction in Virginia. Because of this, Virginia's Consumer Real Estate Settlement Protection Act (CRESPA) requires all settlement agents to register with the Virginia State Bar. The Bar then holds these settlement agents to the highest possible standards. Prior to that time, however, there is work to be done.

As the seller, you have the final determination whether or not to accept an offer. In the best of worlds, you will find a buyer who has enough money, is highly qualified, and is very interested in your home. But in reality, there are often good buyers who may be first-time homebuyers, who are getting a low down payment or nothing-down loan, or are borrowing the earnest money to submit with the offer. We have submitted offers for first-time homebuyers with a promissory note as the earnest money. This is when the buyer promises to produce the earnest money deposit over the course of so many days but prior to closing. We have also submitted offers with minimal earnest money. It is then incumbent on your Realtor® to determine whether minimal earnest money should be a deterrent to the buyer's ability to purchase your home.

The buyer's agent may want to include one or more "extra" clauses in the offer to purchase to cover special requests. For example, they may want to have the carpet professionally steam cleaned prior to closing, and such a clause could be included in the contract. If the buyer is purchasing land on which to build a home, they would probably want to know if a survey, soil tests or other information is available. Again, a clause would be inserted to cover that need. There are so many clauses, and so many special requests by buyers, that to cover them all would be impossible.

Once the offer is submitted to you, there are three possible responses: (1) you can accept the offer as submitted and sign it, officially accepting the offer; (2) you can counter (in essence, rejecting) the offer with put a brand new offer on the table; or (3) you can outright reject the offer.

Once you have accepted the offer without question, do not try to second-guess the process. It is not the time to worry if you accepted too little or gave up too much. If you've done your homework, and you got what you wanted in the deal, be happy. The buyer probably has an agent smart enough to advise them that the offer meets your needs and it was not worthwhile trying to squeeze more out of it.

It is absolutely silly, however, to refuse to respond to a legitimate offer. Hopefully your Realtor® will not let you ignore a good offer. Recently, one of Susan's sellers had a property on the market at $379,000 and an offer came in at $363,000. He reacted to the offer as though it was insulting and would not even respond—this from a man who regularly made very low offers on properties when he was the buyer. Susan told him that ignoring the offer was not an option; he hired her to sell his property and part of his responsibility was to communicate with every potential buyer until they either bought the property or went away. He said, "Fine, then tell them I'm holding out for full price." Susan did. Within an hour, the same buyer submitted a new offer at $376,000, and the seller accepted. There are, however, agents who forget their objectivity, become emotionally involved, and take offers personally. When reviewing a buyer's low offer, we've had listing agents tell us, with all the resentment they can muster, "This is an insult. My seller won't even respond to this." The agent should realize that they are not the seller, *you* are. If there is a viable buyer who wants the property and is capable of buying it, they will run the risk of losing a sale for you.

Finally, although most rejected first offers elicit a counterproposal from the buyer you should beware. Often the first offer is the best. The negotiating process continues until you and the buyers have come to an agreement on the price, terms, inclusions, and exclusions which work for both of you. If the agents and their clients have done their work responsibly, it should be a deal that makes everyone satisfied, even happy. It will be a win/win deal for everyone.

Once you have agreed to accept an offer, you and the buyer will sign a contract within an agreed-upon time. A contract is simply an agreement between two or more people (called *parties*) to do certain things, and in exchange, some form of compensation is paid. In this case, when you and the buyer do what you have agreed to do in the contract, the house will be transferred to the buyer and you will get your money.

Some of Your Responsibilities Are:

- providing the buyer with a property condition disclosure, which is your best representation of the condition of the property and all the fixtures that will be sold to the buyer;
- providing a lead paint disclosure if the property was built before 1978;
- letting the buyer know if there are any material defects with the property (required by Virginia law);
- providing the buyer with declarations and bylaws, covenants and restrictions, homeowners' association financial documents, or any other documents which pertain to any homeowners' association or neighborhood group which might have some say as to what you can and cannot do with your home;
- letting the buyer and certain other people have access to the home for purposes of conducting a home inspection, an appraisal, taking measurements, and so forth;
- answering the buyer's legitimate questions about the house; and
- showing up at the appointed settlement time to sign the documents to transfer title of the property to the buyer.

Some of the Buyer's Responsibilities Are:

- applying for a mortgage loan (if needed) and providing all the information required by the lender to process that loan;

- getting the money necessary to close the purchase—down payment and closing costs;
- providing, and usually paying for, an appraisal to determine the current market value of the property (this is separate from the appraisal that you may have paid for yourself, earlier in the process, to determine the best selling price for your home);
- if negotiated in the offer, conducting an inspection of the property, usually with the help of a professional home inspector, or other qualified professional; and
- showing up at the settlement to take title to the property and pay you the money for your home.

Contingencies

Nearly every contract has contingencies which give one party or the other the right to cancel the contract if certain things about the property are deemed unsatisfactory, or certain obligations are not met. For example, the loan contingency clause requires the buyer to apply for a mortgage by a certain date and to get loan approval by another specific date. If the buyer's lender anticipates problems getting loan approval, it will be up to the buyers to cancel the contract by the loan approval deadline. In that event, the property will go back on the market. In Virginia, the buyer (and seller) has the right to hire an attorney at any time if they feel the need during the transaction.

The buyer and their attorney have the right to review homeowner's association documents, and if the buyer finds those documents unacceptable, they can cancel the contract, and buy another property. Let's look at some of the major contingencies included in nearly every home purchase contract.

The buyer normally has the right to conduct an inspection of your home to determine its condition and everything included in the sale. This contingency gives the buyer the right to ask you to remedy things that may reduce the value of the home, and to terminate the contract if you can't reach an agreement on payment for potential repairs.

Other contingencies can also be built into an offer, the inclusion of which will depend on a variety of circumstances. For example, perhaps the buyer must sell their current home before they will have the money to purchase your home. In this case, they will want a contingency stating that if they cannot sell their existing home, they can terminate your contract. If you are willing to accept such a contingency, you should use it as a bargaining tool—maybe in exchange for taking the home as is—and you should impose a definite time limit.

If there are special problems with the property, the buyer may ask you to address them, and make their offer contingent on their successful resolution. For instance, if a neighbor has an outbuilding or driveway that encroaches on your property, they may ask you to take the necessary steps to eliminate the encroachment. Because you may already have an established relationship with your neighbors, it might be easy for you to accomplish, making the buyer happy at a very small cost.

Some other common contingencies regularly used in Northern Virginia include:

- Testing for Radon;
- The seller finding a home of choice;
- A third party approval (such as a parent helping with the financing);

- Back up contract (in case the 1st buyer decides to void the contract).

Inspection

If you are selling a condominium in a newer project, the buyer may feel comfortable conducting the home inspection themselves. Some of our buyers have plugged a hair dryer into all the electrical outlets to make sure they were working, run the dishwasher, turned on all the burners on the stove, tried the oven, run water in all sinks, baths and toilets to make sure there were no leaks, and checked for other details which could be inspected by observation. Particularly in older properties, many use professional home inspectors. The buyer should review the condominium documents to determine the responsibilities of the homeowners' association. For example, if heat is included in the dues, the association is generally responsible for maintaining heating systems. It is also generally responsible for outside maintenance, including painting, roof replacement, maintenance of common facilities such as a pool or clubhouse, and so on. But if the heating system is separate for each condominium and the individual homeowners are responsible, the buyer must also inspect the heating system. In that case, the buyer might need a professional home inspector.

A good home inspector has been trained in all the systems and details that make up a house. A good home inspection will take from a couple of hours to a full day, depending on the size and complexity of your house. Make sure the buyers know about important positive facts, such as a newly replaced roof, rather than letting an inspector guess that it is five or six years old. Inspectors are not perfect, and the reality is that their inspections are mostly based on visual perceptions.

At the completion of the inspection, the inspector may take the buyer through the home to emphasize what might need attention. Those are things the buyer may want to discuss with you and your Realtor®. The buyer may ask you to remedy some or all of those items. Hopefully the buyer's agent will inform them not to "sweat the small stuff." For example, if all the buyer finds in the home inspection is a bathtub or two that need caulking, furnace filters that need changing, an outside door that needs a new weather seal or some other minor details, the buyer should agree to do the repairs themselves once they move in. However, occasionally the inspector will discover a condition that requires a specialist. For example, they may find a cracked foundation wall that could be due to something more than normal settling. In that case, they might recommend the buyer have a structural engineer inspect the foundation. Other serious issues, from the chimney to the furnace, may require different specialists.

It would be appropriate for the buyer to request that you correct any major problems. If the heat exchanger on the furnace has a leak, it must be replaced, which can be costly. If any appliances do not work, the buyer may ask that they be repaired or replaced. If the roof is in such disrepair or so old that replacement is imminent, the buyer may ask you to have it replaced prior to completing the sale.

When the buyer makes these requests, you can respond in a variety of ways: you can agree to have the problems remedied prior to closing, if you think that the cost to you is reasonable in relation to the sales price; you can refuse on the grounds that the price the buyer negotiated on the house does not leave you enough money to make the corrections; or you may offer to settle with the buyer somewhere in between. If you do not have the cash to fix the furnace, for example, but recognize that it needs repairing, you can offer to compensate the buyer at closing and let the buyer have it repaired after the home is theirs. As long as you and the buyer can resolve the inspection items to your mutual satisfaction and you put the agreement in writing, you can proceed to settlement. If you cannot resolve the issues, the buyer can cancel the contract and move on. In fact, if the buyer finds a serious, ongoing problem (like the foundation wall), the buyer may want to terminate the contract outright.

Title Documents and Easements

The buyer has the right to pick the settlement company to handle the closing of the transaction. In Virginia, this company will coordinate the collection of documents and the eventual collection and disbursement of funds. The settlement company performs the title search and works with the seller to remove any defects on the title. It shows things about the property that may need to be cleared up prior to closing or that might impede the buyer's ability to purchase the home. If there are defects that can not be remedied, oftentimes the title insurance can not be issued. If this is the case, the lender will not fund the buyer's loan.

There are also things on virtually every set of title documents that will remain with the property even after sale. Utility companies which have power, sewer, water and cable lines running to the property will generally have a continuing easement to go onto the land for purposes of repair, replacement or installation of utilities. This is limited to the areas designated on the *plat,* the surveyor's exact drawing of the home site.

An easement is not an actual title to or ownership of property. It is simply a recorded agreement giving access to another person or entity for limited purposes. Local governments might have easements for a variety of reasons, such as access to power poles. Some states may require homeowners in certain communities to set aside extra land to dump snow off the roadway, or in beach communities to allow for public access to the waterfront. An easement may give a neighbor the right to cross your property to get to their own, or to share a driveway if they are otherwise unable to get reasonable access to their home. Or, the buyer may have an easement across a neighbor's land. Easements are very common and should not deter a buyer from purchasing your home. If they have an experienced Realtor®, they should already be informed of this fact.

Common Interest Communities

Until the 1960s, neighborhoods were established and communities grew without a lot of community planning. In older cities, you will often find that homes in the same neighborhood are very different from one another. You may find a ranch house next to a modern house, or a shack next to a mansion. In the mountains you often see an A-frame next to a large traditional-style house. Commercial, residential, and industrial components can be randomly interspersed. Over time, governing authorities (town councils and county governments) have usually developed rules and regulations that give them the authority to approve what is built, to ensure some consistency exists in each neighborhood development, and to designate how homes, stores and industrial development will be separated.

Restrictions on building, imposed by both governments and developers, have flourished in the past 30 years, but for different reasons. Governments want to control growth and developers want to preserve values.

Therefore, depending on the neighborhood, the developer may have filed documents with the governing authority that establish certain guidelines. These are generally called the *covenants, conditions, and restrictions* (CC&Rs) for a neighborhood. Often these documents incorporate a set of architectural guidelines, which may be more or less restrictive than local building codes.

In Virginia, there are two types of documents that are involved in a sale. One is specific to selling condominiums. The other is specific to selling homes located in communities that fall under the Virginia Property Owners' Association Act or POA Act. Each have separate laws governing what kinds of disclosures are required and how this information needs to be reported to a potential buyer.

All of these documents must be provided to the buyer once a contract is ratified, and prior to settlement. It is important for the buyer to review them. In the case of properties falling under the POA Act, it is required by Virginia law for the buyer to review these documents prior to settlement. The restrictions imposed by these documents may be perfectly acceptable to the buyer. For example, some neighborhood associations will not allow anyone to have junk cars parked in front of homes and will not allow the buyer to conduct auto repairs on the property. The restrictions are designed to ensure that only certain types of people would live in the neighborhood—those who like the restrictions. If the buyer happens to be a backyard mechanic, this type of neighborhood may not work.

Some associations restrict the size and number of household pets. Some condominium associations insist that anything stored on a deck (like bicycles) not be visible from the street. For example, an RV owner would be unpleasantly surprised to find out after closing that the covenants prohibited RVs from being parked anywhere on the property. But because restrictions are to be expected when buying a condo or a house in a planned community, this should not affect the sale.

If you are selling a condominium, townhouse, or other property that requires the payment of dues and assessments, you must, by Virginia law, provide the buyer with either a Resale Certificate in the case of a condominium, or an Association Disclosure Packet in the case of a property subject to the POA Act. In addition to a budget, these documents, particularly in the case of a condominium, oftentimes include the minutes of the past two or three meetings, which will help them determine whether the association is financially viable—if it has established reserves to cover major periodic maintenance such as roofs, paved parking areas, and painting. If reserves are not substantial enough, homeowners could be faced with future special assessments. That is, every homeowner is asked to pay a set amount (sometimes amounting to thousands of dollars) to pay for a needed improvement to the whole complex. If the buyer reviews the minutes or places a telephone call to a member of the association board of directors, they can also get information about what the association is planning.

The buyer will have an opportunity to review the Resale Certificate or the Association Disclosure Packet, and it is important for the buyer to voice any objections before the stated deadline. In Virginia, that time period is 3 calendar days from receipt of the documents or if mailed, within 6 days after the postmarked date. If there is anything they cannot live with, they have the right to terminate the contract within a reasonable period of time (usually designated in the purchase contract).

The Appraisal

If the buyer is having part of the purchase financed with a mortgage loan, the loan will generally be contingent on a satisfactory appraisal of value. The buyer has the option of including an appraisal contingency if they are paying cash, but it will be required by their lender if they are financing. This appraisal is the same as the one you may have had done yourself prior to determining the sale price, except that it is paid for by the buyer.

Again, an appraisal is a process whereby a licensed professional examines your home, reviews similar properties that have been sold recently, and gives an opinion of the fair-market value of your property. However, at this phase, the appraiser also looks at the contract in place between you and the buyer. If they determine the contract sets a price that is fairly close to the value established by looking at comparable sold properties, they will most likely establish a fair-market value at or close to your contract price.

If your contract price is substantially different, then the fair-market value may be either higher or lower. If the appraisal is higher than what you have agreed to sell the home for, you should not be too concerned, especially if you did your homework. More likely than not, you and your Realtor® negotiated a very good deal. If it comes in lower (even by $1), and you have allowed the buyer to make the appraisal a contingency in the contract, they have the right to terminate the contract. The contract can be kept intact, however, by one of three agreements: (1) They agree to pay a larger down payment (because their lender will only lend based on the appraised value); (2) you agree to lower the contract price; or (3) you and the buyers agree to settle someplace in between.

In Virginia, the current appraisal contingency attempts to keep the contract between the seller and the buyer alive by first giving the seller the option of lowering the sales price to appraised value. If the seller agrees to lower the sales price to the appraised value, the contract will go forward. If the seller does not agree to lower the sales price to the appraised value, then both parties can negotiate until they reach mutually acceptable terms. If there is no meeting of the minds, then the contract can be voided by either party.

Financing

In most states the buyer loses their earnest money deposit if they default on the contract, and additional penalties could be imposed. If they are financing the purchase, they will usually request a contingency for such a case. In other words, the buyer would be given a certain amount of time for the lender to approve their loan within certain established parameters. In some states, if the buyer does not have full loan approval at terms acceptable to them by the loan approval deadline, they must provide you with written notice in order to terminate the contract.

If the buyer is having difficulty getting the loan they want and a lender suggests another loan that will work, you and your agent or attorney may want to negotiate a limited extension of the contract. Whether you agree to cooperate will depend on how interested you are in continuing to work with the buyer. If the buyer does not terminate the contract under a loan contingency and subsequently fails to qualify for a loan and cannot continue with the purchase, they are considered in default.

It is critically important that you, your attorney and/or your Realtor® be cognizant of all contract deadlines and who must perform what obligations by each deadline. In doing so, you will be able to protect your rights under the contract, including your right to earnest money if the contract is wrongfully terminated.

In Virginia, the law requires releases to be signed by both parties before any earnest money deposit can be dispersed. If either party refuses to sign the release, the deposit will remain with whoever is holding it, and cannot be released until directed by a court of competent jurisdiction.

9. Preparing for Uncle Sam

A dear friend referred Susan to us. After a brief face-to-face meeting, we decided she was a Realtor® we wanted to work with. We couldn't have made a wiser choice.

Susan began by listening. She let us tell her what we were looking for in a new home, what our time table was, what we wanted to spend, and how involved we wanted her to be. Only after this did she begin to make suggestions that were suited to our needs. While we were not first-time homebuyers, we were by no means experts. Susan gave us straight answers to direct questions. She also served us in good faith, explaining things we needed to know, even if we didn't know enough to ask about them.

Our experience was so positive that when it came time to sell our home and purchase another, we called Susan. She brings to her work all the qualities one looks for, not just in a Realtor®, but also in a person. She is knowledgeable without condescension. She is pro-active without being pushy. She is enthusiastic without being unrealistic. She offers her opinion without imposing her will. But more importantly, she is there when you need her.

—Cathy Hoefler and Doug Dunn,
South Riding, Virginia

Whether you're self-employed, a wage earner or own your own business, you know that Uncle Sam, through the Internal Revenue Service, is your silent partner. It's no different when you sell your home. When you sell it for more than you paid, you create a taxable gain. However, just as you were able to take deductions on your tax return for the interest you paid while living in your home, Uncle Sam has created some wonderful tax benefits when you sell your home.

Please be aware we are *not* providing tax advice. As we said at the beginning of this book, we have tried to be as accurate as possible when it comes to what works and what doesn't in selling a home. In this section we will talk about how the tax laws work in your favor as a home seller. We have attempted to ensure that everything said here is accurate and relevant, but laws change, circumstances vary, and there is always the possibility for error. Using the guidance offered here, along with your selection of a competent tax professional, whether a Certified Public Account or a tax attorney, you should feel confident in selling real estate and legally avoiding taxes on any gain you may have created. If your situation is complicated by any of a number of factors—if the property is classed as a business, farm, ranch or multi-unit residence—please consult a tax professional who specializes in that area.

Let's start with the first tax advantage: It used to be that if you sold your home and purchased another, all gain from the appreciation in the value of your old home could be transferred to your new one without owing current income or capital gains taxes, provided you rolled that gain over into a new home within 24 months of selling your old one. This was under IRS Code Section 1034, prior to the Taxpayer Relief Act (TRA) of 1997. Section 1034 also replaced IRS Code Section 121, which was designed for taxpayers who were over age 55 and allowed a $500,000 exclusion for married couples or a $250,000 exclusion for a single person on the sale of their principal residence. Now you no longer need to buy another house of equal or greater value to claim the exclusion.

You can take advantage of the new law over and over again (although not more than once every two years), but there are certain guidelines. First, the property must be your principal residence and not a second home or rental property. Second, it may be a detached house, a mobile home, a co-op apartment or a condominium, but you cannot have more than one principal residence at the same time. Third, you must have lived in the house for at least two of the last five years prior to the sale. There is even a benefit to a spouse who is not living in the house at the time of the sale; they can claim up to $250,000 of tax-free profits, provided they too lived in the home for two of the last five years. This also applies to two co-owners who are not married, as long as they meet the occupancy rules.

Even if one spouse dies, these tax benefits are available. The surviving spouse, whether widow or widower, is allowed to claim the full $500,000 exclusion if the home is sold in the same year that the spouse died.

Section 1034 eliminates most of the record-keeping requirements if you know that your gain will be less than $250,000. By the way, the gain you are allowed to exclude is the lesser of your gain or $250,000. In other words, if your gain is $100,000 on the sale of your home, you do not get to take a $250,000 deduction. In the past, your escrow company had to file a Form 1099-S and report your taxable gain to the IRS. This is no longer required. However, if you take a loss on the sale of your home, you can't deduct that loss; remember, you had been getting an interest deduction.

Investment Property Relief

Tax deferral is also available when you sell a rental home or an apartment building if you follow the guidelines in IRS Code Section 1031. This is called a *1031 tax-*

deferred exchange, and is a powerful way to create wealth through real estate. You can sell investment property and transfer all of the gain to another larger investment property and defer the taxes that would have been due on a straight sale.

Here's how it works: An investor/taxpayer can avoid the taxes on the sale of investment property and qualify for *exchange* treatment if the property was held as investment property, or for use in a trade or business, and was exchanged from property that was like that which was sold. This is called *like-kind.* However, prior to the sale of the old property the seller must enter into an exchange agreement with a *qualified intermediary.* This person or company structures the exchange transaction to meet all of the IRS Code requirements.

What Is a Qualified Intermediary?

A qualified intermediary is also known as a *facilitator* or *accommodator.* This is a person or company who holds the funds from your sale and structures the transaction to meet IRS requirements. Unfortunately, there are no federal or state laws that govern an accommodator. Anyone can claim to qualify; however, it cannot be anyone close to you, such as your accountant, attorney, banker, employee or family member. You must confirm that they are qualified, that they have the knowledge, experience and credentials to perform for you. Also, since they will hold your money, you want to be sure they don't take an extended trip to a country without an extradition treaty.

Ask the accommodator if they pay interest on your funds. Ask for their fee structure and whether there are extra charges if you require additional consultations. Verify that they are members of the national organization for qualified intermediaries, the Federation of Exchange Accommodators (FEA). Confirm that they carry an independent bond issued by an insurance company that specializes in this type of coverage. This is one of the most important items. You don't want to be left empty-handed if your money is stolen by the intermediary or one of their employees.

IRS Guidelines

There are three basic guidelines set out by the IRS to qualify for exchange treatment. First, the purchase price of the replacement property must be equal to or greater than the property you sold.

Second, the debt on the replacement property, the mortgage, must be equal to or greater than the debt held on the property you sold. There should be no relief of your debt.

Third, all of the net proceeds, the total amount you received for your property, must be used to buy the replacement property.

If you don't follow these three guidelines, you can still complete the exchange, but you may have taxes to pay. As an example, if you hold out $100,000 from the exchange (this is called *boot*), it will be taxed. When attempting a partial exchange it is crucial you get competent tax advice.

Like-Kind Property

Like-kind refers to the type of property involved in an exchange. According to the IRS this is "any property held for productive use in a trade or business or held for investment purposes." As an example, you can exchange an apartment building for a commercial building, or a rental single-family home for an apartment building or a shopping center. Even raw or vacant land and a leasehold for 30 years or more count under exchange rules.

The following property is not considered real estate, and therefore does not count as exchange property: money, stocks, bonds, and notes. Also, limited partnerships and your primary residence do not qualify.

Time Frame

Most exchanges occur as delayed exchanges, and there are two key deadlines to keep in mind. The first is the 45-day period to identify the property you want to acquire after the close of escrow on your property. The second is the 180-day period by which you must close escrow on your replacement property. There are no exceptions or extensions.

You have two choices when it comes to identifying your replacement property. The first is the *three-property rule,* and the second is the *200 percent rule*. The three-property rule allows you to identify up to three properties that you want to acquire as an exchange. You may purchase one or all of the properties to complete your exchange as long as they follow the IRS guidelines described earlier. If you choose to purchase more than three properties, you must qualify under the 200 percent rule, which allows you to identify as many properties as you want as long as the total market value of all the identified properties is less than 200 percent of the value of the sold property. You will need to complete an *identification notice* for your qualified intermediary to comply with the IRS rules.

Most often, when sellers consider a tax-deferred exchange they are dealing with large amounts of money. Competent advice is suggested because the penalty for failure to follow the rules is substantial. Please consult qualified professionals.

Section II

Buying Your Next Home

Buying Your Next Home

It is sometimes difficult to balance selling your home while trying to buy a new home. The timing is often hard to gauge. Should you wait until you have a contract before you start looking? And if you wait too long, could you face a period of "homelessness"? Don't panic. Like all other aspects of buying and selling real estate, planning is everything. Make a backup plan for what you will do if your present house is sold before you find a new one. Or conversely, make a plan for how you will deal with the possibility of owning two homes for a period of time. Your choices should depend on your time frame and your budget.

In general, we recommend waiting to look for your new home until you are under contract with a buyer, for several reasons. First, if you find a new home before you sell your current one you could be faced with two mortgages, which few of us can really afford—not to mention that the burden could affect the financing of your new home. Although you can use the equity in one home to finance the other, many banks will charge you a higher rate and you will have to refinance as soon as your house is sold.

Second, if the idea of two mortgages is unrealistic for your financial situation, you could get panicked and unnecessarily sell below-market. In the end this could cost you much more than the price of interim housing. Although you could ask the seller of the home you have your heart set on to make the purchase contingent on the sale of your current home, most sellers are unwilling to do so, due to the high risk it carries. This contingency could be particularly difficult to get in a hot housing market. And if your house remains unoccupied, you could pay substantially higher insurance rates, sometimes as much as four times your old rate, because vacant homes have a much higher risk of vandalism and arson.

Another option is to rent your house until it sells, but houses with renters are generally harder to sell. Renters don't necessarily take the same care of your house as you would, so it never "shows" as well. In addition, buyers are sometimes reluctant to deal with the possibility of having to evict someone if the tenant refuses to leave after the sale.

It really is best to sell first and have a game plan if you don't find something right away. Although potential "double moves" are expensive, you can try to lease back your sold house for a short period of time, or put your belongings in storage and stay with friends or relatives. And, of course, you can rent some form of short-term housing. Since your Realtor® knows your needs best, they can often be a very good source for finding affordable short-term housing, especially if you have children or pets. Although these choices may seem daunting or expensive, if you plan ahead they may save you the anxiety of owning two homes. Or worse yet, selling in a panic at below market price.

Another rule of thumb to follow is to buy first when prices are heading up, and sell first when they are heading down. That way you are in the best position to get a good deal in the market. Like we've said before, planning is the key to making a smooth purchase or sale of property.

10. Play the Field and Lose the Game

> Just wanted to send you a quick note regarding my recent purchase in Arlington. *I love it!* I am so happy here. It is so quiet. I can't believe that I rented for so long. No buyer's remorse! I have pulled this place together with new furniture, new paint, and I updated all the light fixtures and hardware. I love coming home! Thanks for all your help!
>
> —Jen Marsho, Arlington, Virginia

Now that you are under contract with a buyer, it's time to find your new home. Perhaps you've been looking already, checking out homes on the Internet or going to open houses. But although you know to use a Realtor® to sell your home, now that it's your turn to buy, do you plan on using a Realtor®?

If you are like many sellers, you may be anxious to find your new home, so you have been calling on ads or for-sale signs, going to open houses, and talking to agents to whom you have been referred. But generally, you have avoided committing to one, usually on the basis that you don't want to be pressured—especially if you haven't yet sold your home. But why play the field? You've already found a great Realtor® to sell your home, and maybe they can help you buy a new one.

Naturally, if you had a good experience with your agent in the sale, you would want to consider the same person to help you buy your new home. Not all Realtors® represent both buyers and sellers, but it's always a good place to start, especially if you are moving in the same area.

If you are working with one Realtor® who knows you won't hop around from one to the next, they will become as committed to you as you are to them. They will become "your" Realtor®, and they will be working for you. They will likely work to help you get qualified for financing, and when that "hot" property comes on the market, guess who they're going to call? Believe me, it won't be the person who happened to stop in for an hour last weekend, it will be the buyer to whom they are committed—it will be you. After all, you are giving them a substantial amount of business and they will want to bring to your attention any property they can find that fits your needs. If it's a great deal, all the better.

We've sold numerous properties where our buyer was the only person to see the house. We try to check new listings regularly, and also watch the newspaper classifieds for homes being sold by owners. Sometimes we see a property that is obviously underpriced, or perhaps "priced for a quick sale." It then becomes imperative to get our buyer into the property before anyone else sees it, because we know it will go fast. We're off with a quick call to the buyer to let them know, "We've got one." We can usually write an offer to purchase or a contract that same day. We know the timing of your sale and we know when you need to find that new home.

We don't get paid until we produce a sale. There is not a lot of loyalty in this business, and there are a lot of short-term thinkers—people who will unknowingly lose thousands of future dollars to save a thousand today. You will find that two-way loyalty pays off. The key is selecting the right agent.

But what if you are moving to a new area and need to find a home? Obviously, you need to find someone who can represent your interests as a buyer. Well, we have some suggestions. One good bet is to look for a Realtor® who holds the designation of "Accredited Buyer Agent (ABR)". If your own personal agent can't represent you because you are looking in another area, your Realtor® should be able to recommend a top-notch professional in your target area.

Usually when you enlist the services of a buyer's agent, you will be working with a Realtor® who will represent your interests as a sort of personal representative. This is known as an agency relationship.

Agency

When you work with a buyer's agent, you will often enter into a representation contract. A buyer-agency contract is a contract between the buyer (you) and the Realtor®, and it works two ways. First, the Realtor® becomes your agent and is obligated to represent your best interests. Second, the contract represents your commitment to the Realtor® and says that you will work exclusively with them. This agreement means that when you see a sign on a property, you will not call the listing agent yourself to negotiate a deal, nor will you go into a property that is for-sale-by-owner to do the same. Instead, you will call your agent and ask them to get you information on the property. You now have an agent; use them. The whole purpose of this exercise is to get you the best deal possible. If you have selected a good agent, you should recognize they have the experience and the skills necessary to represent you effectively. It takes a modicum of trust to see that play out, and now is when your Realtor® earns their commission.

There are a few items you should pay particular attention to in a buyer-agency contract. In some states, most are already part of the standard contract, but elsewhere, this may not be the case. Before you sign, at least discuss the following topics.

Confidentiality

If you are to be represented effectively, it is imperative that the agent keep confidential any information they learn about you. In particular, your financial situation, willingness to accept concessions, and motivating factors for the purchase should not be revealed, except as a valid negotiating tool with your prior consent.

In addition, you have a right to be assured that confidential information remains confidential even after you have bought your home or after your contract with the agent has expired or been terminated in any way. If you make an offer on an in-house transaction (where the seller is also represented by the brokerage representing you), your information should remain just as confidential as when negotiating for a property listed by another firm.

Scope of Work

The contract will contain a description of what type of property your agent is instructed to seek for you. Make sure the description fits your needs. If you are looking specifically for a residence, make sure the language limits the search to that. Do not accept language that says "any property." If you are considering purchasing a home from a family member or friend, you may ask to have that property excluded from the contract; however, you may want to ask your agent what they would charge to handle that transaction for you. Pitfalls can still exist and in fact can be more serious and more heart-wrenching when dealing with someone close to you. Many close relationships have been damaged or ruined when friends and relatives have done business together. It's usually not because of a lack of good intentions, but when objectivity is lost, personal feelings get exaggerated and hurt and the process erodes. We've worked on numerous deals where family members and close friends were involved, and we have found that it becomes vitally important to ensure a win/win deal for everyone involved.

Many buyer agents typically write contracts for six months. Often we work with buyers of second homes, and the process involves communicating while they are in another city or state. We will coordinate property showings with their vacations to the area, and sometimes they buy properties we've recommended sight unseen. Even when working with locals, using a six-month representation period makes sense.

This long period can be scary. What if you decide you don't like your agent? What if your plans change? The simplest answer is to ask for a cancellation clause. Always include a clause that says that either party, the buyer or agent, may cancel the contract for any reason whatsoever by providing written notice to the other party. While they may ask for ten-day advance notice, people who are not compatible should not have to work together. If your Realtor® is willing to give you this "out" in your contract, you can bet they are confident in their ability to represent you effectively. Keep in mind that you are not able to cancel a contract for a property on which you are already negotiating, and every contract will have what is called a "holdover" clause that entitles your agent to a commission if, after your contract has terminated, you buy a property the agent showed you.

The entire contract should be designed to be fair to both parties. It is fair to be able to cancel a contract when two people cannot work together. It is not fair to have someone do a lot of work for you and then cancel. You should be able to determine in the first or second meeting with your Realtor® whether or not you are compatible. Don't spend several weeks or months together and then decide to go with someone else.

Again, the bottom line is that if you do the same research to find a buyer's agent as you did to find your seller's agent, you should have the right person to help you find your next home (again, refer to the credentials mentioned in Chapter 2). If you are moving in the same area and can rely on the relationship with your present Realtor®, you are in a great position, but a buyer's agent is still the next best thing.

11. Mortgage Rate Deals

In a casual conversation, I expressed to Susan my interest in purchasing a property rather than paying rent. Susan took the time to explain to me the benefits of owning my own home. When she realized money was an issue, she helped me to weigh the pros and cons of renting versus owning. She took her time to show me all the possibilities from rental properties, renting to own, and properties on the market to buy. The year Susan spent with me in the beginning stages not only shows her concern for finding her clients the perfect property but also the dedication and time she invests to educate them on the real estate market.

Once I made my decision to buy, Susan suggested I meet with a lender to see exactly what I could afford. This helped in narrowing our search. As we looked at properties, Susan carefully noted what features interested me the most. She came prepared with listings that met my needs and made every property viewing experience a comfortable one.

When the right home was finally found, Susan rushed to her office to write the contract. It was a tough contract to negotiate, but through her endless support, skills, knowledge, and dedication, Susan made it a ratified contract. Settlement was stress free, organized, and enjoyable.

After writing my first mortgage payment, I felt it necessary to thank Susan once again for the "world class service" and for finding me the perfect home.

—Alana Stanley, Alexandria, Virginia

Real estate is such a great investment! There is probably nowhere else where you can leverage so much with so little. You can purchase a $400,000 home with $5,000. If that home goes up in value $40,000 (or 10 percent) in a year, you're return on your $5,000 investment is 800 percent. Sound too good to be true? It's not. People do it every day. The best place to start investing in life is in your personal residence. If you are considering renting—don't do it! Renting is a losing proposition. All the money goes out and none comes back to you. As a homeowner, you get an appreciating asset and the tax advantage of deducting the interest portion of your payment. But for now let's talk about how to get the majority of the money to buy your next home.

First, you need to find a lender. Make sure you have a lender that specializes in providing loans for the type of purchase you are making. If you are buying a home, you will use a residential mortgage lender, and if you are buying land, with certain exceptions, you will probably use a bank. A mortgage lender can do land loans if you are buying a lot and plan to build a home on it immediately. Many mortgage companies now offer what is called a *one-time close, construction-to-perm* loan, which will help you finance the land purchase, provide the construction financing, and then provide the permanent financing once the home is built.

Although we discussed lenders in regard to the sale of your home, once you are ready to buy it is your turn to find financing with the best terms possible. Whether you use a loan officer at a bank, a broker or a mortgage lender recommended by your Realtor®, you will want to make sure that they work hard to get you the best deal they can. At the end of the day, when you commit to a loan, the lender makes a commission. Make sure that they earn it!

In all states, banks are regulated by various government agencies in their practice of providing home loans. However, in Ken's state of Colorado, mortgage lenders and mortgage brokers do not have to be licensed. This means anyone can get into the business, say they are a mortgage lender, do a lousy job, and you have no recourse through a licensing body. Even though many states require lenders to be licensed, lenders vary widely in honesty and integrity. Therefore, you must be diligent in selecting your lender and loan officer as they can hold the key to your purchase. Be sure to ask your Realtor® about the licensing requirements for mortgage lenders, mortgage brokers, and loan officers in your area.

In Virginia, mortgage brokers are required to be licensed by the Virginia State Corporation Commission. Mortgage lenders also need to be licensed, but if they make 3 or fewer mortgage loans in any period of 12 consecutive months, they are exempt from the licensing requirements as well as the other provisions of the mortgage lender and broker act. As mentioned earlier regarding Realtors® who don't work a lot, these mortgage lenders either just got started or can't get enough business to survive and are on their way into another profession. Susan recommends steering clear of them and finding a licensed broker or lender. Individual loan officers working for a company, such as a bank, do not need to be licensed.

A loan officer is much like a real estate agent: You may be referred to one by a friend, have a family member in the business or happen to meet one by accident. Just remember that not all loan officers are created equal. A good Realtor® will have a short list of lenders and loan officers who have proven they know what they are doing, only make promises they can keep, don't spring last-minute surprises, have a substantial menu of loans to cover most situations, and have competitive rates and costs. You want to avoid last-minute surprises like finding out a day or two before you are supposed to close that the underwriter has a list of conditions which will be impossible to meet prior to closing.

Beware of lenders who advertise low rates in major newspapers or on the Internet. Purchasers have often started their loan applications before they met and retained a quality Realtor® to assist in their home purchases. In many cases where the clients stayed with that lender, they have regretted their selection. Typically, something goes wrong. The most common problems are interest rate increases, disregarding good faith estimates, hidden fees, processing delays, and lost documents.

We keep lists of lenders who meet our criteria, and a good Realtor® will also be familiar with the basics of loan processing and the types of loans available so they can provide guidance as you work with the lender and can tell if the person you are working with is knowledgeable. However, many agents simply refer you to a lender and stay completely out of the process. We feel teamwork will get more deals done and we tend to stay involved and brainstorm unique possibilities with our buyers and their lenders.

In a contrasting example, a recent first-time homebuyer, whom we'll call Bob, started out with a lender Susan had recommended. Then Bob found a "great" rate on the Internet and chose to go with the Internet lender instead.

Remember the earlier warning? Bob decided he wanted to switch his loan to the lender who quoted the lowest rates. Clients always have the right to choose their own lenders, but we do caution them when we are not familiar with a lender they choose. We cannot vouch for that lender's service, competence or knowledge. Often we interview a lender to determine the viability of the loan program they're offering and to get a sense of how well that lender can represent the client.

Because Bob found his lender on the Internet, the lender was from another state and therefore was not familiar with Virginia's appraisal procedures. The lender was supposed to order the appraisal but never did, thinking that it was Bob's responsibility. Unfortunately this was not discovered until the day before closing. The closing had to be postponed and of course by this time Bob's rate lock had expired. But thanks to Susan's connections, she was able to get him a new loan through the original lender with a similar rate to the original loan's and in the end everyone was happy.

A good faith estimate is a form your lender provides you that shows the lender's regular charges, along with the other anticipated closing costs involved with the loan. It utilizes those figures to estimate the total amount of cash you will need to buy your house, and calculates your approximate monthly payment. Some lenders will insist they cannot provide a good faith estimate until you have a property under contract or in escrow. That's just not true. Good faith estimates are simply that—estimates—and they can be prepared quickly and easily. In fact, some lenders we work with will prepare several, one for each loan scenario they are discussing with you. It assists you in comparing those loans so you can decide which one makes the most sense for you and your situation.

It also gives you something to compare with other lenders if you happen to be shopping for the best rates and costs. If one lender charges, for example, a $450 loan processing fee, and another charges $150, and the rates and other fees are the same, you might want to spend more time with the lender who charges less. But do not let these fees be the only reason for selecting a lender. Consider what happened to Bob. A good mortgage broker is worth their weight in gold.

You should also get a good faith estimate on two other occasions: (1) when you have a property under contract, and your Realtor® provides a copy of that contract to the lender; and (2) when you change loan programs, either because you don't qualify for the one you started with, or you decide on a different plan. Once you are under contract, many of the items that were estimated on the first good faith estimate are known, so the estimate is more accurate and closer to reality.

Last-Minute Fees

Occasionally, one of our clients decides to use a lender we haven't recommended. In one case, a couple decided to work with a lender who was renting a home from one of their parents. The lender promised to cut his origination fee in half because of the relationship. Oftentimes, lenders will charge a 1.0 percent loan origination fee. That fee is generally split between loan officers and the mortgage company they work for. In this case, the lender either gave up their portion of that fee, or worked it out with their boss to discount the deal. At any rate, when Ken compared his good faith estimate with other lenders, the reduced fee made the difference. Their loan was going to be about $140,000, so a 1.0 percent fee would have been $1,400. They saved $700 by going with this lender, all other things being equal.

Ken met with the lender and told him if he really took care of the clients, he would get other referrals from him. The lender was just getting established in the area, and he was eager for the new business. However, it took him longer to process the loan than he thought, and Ken did not have a settlement statement until the actual day of closing. Ken called him and the title company to bring something to their attention—the fact that there was a 1.0 percent loan origination fee on the statement rather than 0.5 percent—and asked for a correction. But this loan officer insisted he had met with the clients, and because they had not locked in their rates, and rates had gone up somewhat, he took a full origination fee rather than increase the rate.

Ken asked to see the new good faith estimate that he should have provided if this were true. He said he did not provide one, but the clients understood the new loan terms. The clients insisted there was no such agreement, and at the closing table they were faced with a dilemma. They had to close with the charges as they appeared, or get the lender to write them a check for the 0.5 percent difference, or walk away and refuse to close on the home. They closed, and did not get a refund from the lender. They were angry with him but happy to be in their new home. That lender has never received a referral from Ken, and within a few months he was out of business, or at least gone from the area. He certainly does not rent from the clients' parents anymore.

Loan Types and Interest Rates

There are a variety of loan types available, and the loan program you select will depend first on your ability to qualify and then on your right to select one over another.

A starting place regarding your ability to qualify for a mortgage loan is the quality of your credit report. Every lender uses the FICO score, which stands for the company who created the scoring formula: Fair Isaac Company. They are a third party who provides the score to a potential lender. The lender does not calculate the score, but uses it to establish a borrower's credit worthiness. Until recently, the components of this scoring system were kept secret, but it's been announced that consumers will be able to get information about their score at www.myFICO.com. In general, they use different models and adjust the score depending on various factors, such as the amount of credit, the level of credit cards with no balances, cards with high balances, bankruptcy, payment patterns, and so on.

At the current time, a score over 700 is excellent. Scores of 620 or above would normally allow you to qualify for A or A+ quality loans. These have the lowest interest rates and the most favorable terms. If we hypothetically use mortgage rates of 7 percent as the best available, a person with a score over 620 would qualify for that rate. Scores below 620 would normally put you in what is called a "sub-prime" category, also called "B" or "C" loans. The interest rate would depend on a variety of information specific to your credit report, but could be as high as 14 percent in today's market. The rules vary considerably between lenders on sub-prime loans. A note on future FICO scores. It has been announced by the three credit bureaus that the scoring system (to be called VantageScore) will be standardized into a format similar to grades in school. By using A represents a score between 901-990, B represents a score between 801 to 900, and so on, they feel it will provide lenders and consumers alike with a much more comprehensible system. As of this writing, we are not sure when this will go into effect.

In addition to the money the borrower would pay for doing a credit check, getting title insurance, and paying escrow charges and appraisal fees, there is a cost to get most mortgage loans: *points*. Points refer to the cost of purchasing a loan. One point represents 1 percent of the loan balance. On a $100,000 loan this would be $1,000 to purchase the loan. If a credit score puts someone in the B or C range, the points could rise to 4, meaning it could cost up to $4,000 to purchase a loan. Other fees could rise from $275 to process the same paperwork for a typical A borrower to $650 for a B or C borrower.

Certain loans are specially targeted for first-time homebuyers and offer features such as low down payment (as little as nothing down), competitive interest rates, and the ability to have a cosigner or receive down payment assistance from another source. There are so many loan variables that it would be impossible to discuss them all here.

At the time of this writing, second-home loans are available for 10 percent down with interest rates as low as on primary residences. Investment loans can be obtained for as little as 10 percent down (though 20 percent or more is most common), and the interest rates are somewhat higher.

The general rule is that the more risk you ask a mortgage company to assume, the tougher the rules will be. Government guaranteed loans (e.g., FHA, VA) take some of the burden off the lender, so they can keep the rules easier for you to meet. But conventional loans (anything not guaranteed by an agency of the federal government) tend to follow this formula: The more money you put down, and the better qualified you are to repay the loan, the more likely the mortgage company will be willing to give you good terms and rates.

Interest rates are around the lowest they have been in more than 20 years. The political and economic climate in this country have conspired to produce 30-year fixed rates that have hovered in the 6.0 percent to 7.5 percent range since 1998. It's at the point where nearly anyone with decent credit and a job can buy a home. You can't always get exactly what you want the first time, but owning, saving, and taking advantage of a growing market may give you the ability to take your increased equity every couple of years and trade into a better home. And maybe you are someone who is doing just that.

Your Credit

As discussed above, in the past it was hard to be an informed consumer in the mortgage arena, because much of the personal credit information used by lenders was unavailable to you. You couldn't find out either your credit score or the criteria used to develop these scores. Consequently, consumers were unable to take proactive steps to improve their credit. Luckily, in the very recent past this has changed. The federal government has now passed a law that requires credit bureaus to release both your three-agency credit report score (FICO) and the bureaus' rating criteria upon requests from consumers. For a small fee you can now obtain this information, or as discussed previously you can contact www.myFICO.com.

There are also credit repair agencies that work with consumers to raise their FICO scores. These agencies work with credit companies regularly, so they understand how to fix mistakes and how consumers can rearrange or repair their own credit, possibly raising their scores as much as 40 to 100 points. This process can even be as quick as a few short weeks for people who need quick credit fixes.

There are also many federal agencies designed to help home buyers. They can help with home loans, credit counseling, and even down-payment assistance. But beware of nonprofit credit counseling services. Although these services can consolidate debts for people who have trouble paying their bills, credit counseling is often looked at in the same light as bankruptcy when it comes to credit bureau scoring.

12. Loan Abuses

Yesterday, Andrea and I went to an open house on Taney about a block from our house. We wanted to get decoration and landscaping ideas. The listing Realtor was familiar with our place. He referred to us as the 'steal deal.' He said our house should have gone for about $565,000 last summer, and as you know, we paid $510,000. He also said that it would fetch at least $550,000 today, assuming we had done nothing to it.

I can't tell you how happy I was! Thank you for finding us a great home at a fantastic value. We just love our place. We'd never sell it!

—Andrea Piani and John M. Wilhelm, Jr., CPA,
Alexandria, Virginia

Due to the fact that buyers never really know the exact amount of their loan or closing costs until they are at the closing table, there can be both the appearance and unfortunately the reality of loan abuse. Although this has changed somewhat in the last few years due to both truth in lending statements and the emergence of standardized closing costs, this is an area where you must make sure you protect yourself.

One reason for these recent changes is the current competitive market. A competitive market works to your advantage if you know how to make it work for you. First, regardless of your credit, in a competitive market it pays to shop around. Look for companies that offer a locked-in rate and standardized closing costs. This will avoid eleventh-hour changes.

You are also entitled by law to a truth-in-lending disclosure that should give you a fairly accurate reflection of your loan payments and the closing costs. Although these are never completely accurate, they are a helpful reflection of the loan and fees.

If your loan is for less than $417,000 (approximately), it is considered a conforming loan and therefore you can qualify for the best rates. If your credit is good, make sure that you look for *conforming,* not *jumbo* loans to get the best deal in this market.

Another way you can protect yourself is by not just knowing who your lender is, but finding out ahead of time who will be servicing your loan. Servicing is frequently sold. Even though you pick a particular lender, after you sign the mortgage you may not have any control over the service. The "servicer" receives your payments, keeps records, gives late fees, follows up on delinquent payments, and handles your complaints. Often the service you receive from these companies is less than desirable, since they have less invested in your business than the actual lender. But you can take some steps to control the level of service you receive.

If you have complaints about your servicer, you should send a written complaint, separate from your payment, to the lender's customer service department. If they do not respond within 20 business days (as they are required to under Section 6 of the Real Estate Settlement Procedures Act [RESPA]), file a complaint with HUD or the Consumer Protection Division of your state's attorney general's office. Don't just take abusive practices by servicers.

Also be aware of general predatory practices. For instance, it is now illegal for Realtors® and lenders to mark up the price of services that they don't provide, such as appraisals and credit reports. The best way to make sure you get what you are promised is to carefully review every document before signing it. You are the customer and mortgages are a competitive market. Be sure to demand the service you deserve.

13. Finding Your Next Home

We wanted to thank you for your hard work, attention to detail, amazing customer service, and your ability to go as far as necessary to help with the complex purchase of our home from our landlord. Since we were first-time homebuyers, we wanted to be represented by a professional. You not only helped us with our financing, but you also put together a realistic offer that made sense to our landlord and was a good deal for us. We particularly appreciated your suggestion to get quotes on doing the upgrades that were desperately required and then figuring out a way to roll that cost into our offer so our mortgage would cover the renovations.

We are so thrilled with our new home and we owe it all to you. Thank you for your superb, Realtor®-oriented performance.

—Matt and Tina Lloyd, Fairfax City, Virginia

Once you have established a relationship with your Realtor® and have your lender on board, you can look for a home with a much better perspective on what you can afford. Whether you are a first-time homebuyer, looking for a second home or building your real estate investment portfolio, knowledge brings understanding and control to the process. You will also be in a better position when making an offer because you are already preapproved for your loan.

The Search

Your Realtor® will first select homes for you to see from the Multiple Listing Service (MLS). However, an agent is not limited to the MLS. They will probably be aware of new-home construction projects and might peruse the newspaper classifieds or otherwise be aware of homes being sold directly by owners. Occasionally, they may have knowledge of a home or two that the owners have not absolutely decided to sell, but who are considering it. In addition, you might see open house signs or other signs on homes that appeal to you. A word of caution: Once you have selected a Realtor® and have an agreement to work together, if you see a sign on a house for sale, *do not* call on the sign. Call your Realtor® instead and ask them to do the research, let you know the details, and set a showing if appropriate. Also, ask them how you should handle yourself in open houses. Keep in mind that the listing agent sitting at the open house or named on a front-lawn signpost usually represents the seller, and would like nothing more than to claim you as "their" buyer.

The homes selected by your Realtor® should generally encompass your stated parameters, including price range, number of bedrooms and baths, general size, garage and other physical attributes. They will be in your preferred neighborhoods, communities or school districts, and will have other characteristics you have indicated are important. As you look, you may find you cannot put all the things you want together in one package. You can get the home you want, but not in the right school district, and so on. You may have to refine your search several times. If you stick to the price parameters established between you, your lender, and your Realtor®, then you may have to give up some of your preferences. If you are unwilling to give anything up, then you will have to take another look at financing—bringing in a family member to cosign, working with a partner or looking for properties in which the seller will carry all or part of the financing.

Even if you believe that the home you are purchasing is your dream home and that you will never leave it, listen to your Realtor®'s advice about which homes will have better resale value in the future. As we mentioned, many clients have traded up to better homes, often several times more than they ever imagined.

Recently, a past client approached Ken. When this couple bought their home, they swore they would live in it for 10 years or longer—this was exactly where they wanted to be. It was less than two years later, and they wanted him to list their home for sale. But they had second thoughts, because it would cost them an extra thousand dollars to sell. They reminded Ken that when they bought, he said, "I'll bet you a thousand dollars you will not be in this home five years from now. In fact, you will probably move on in less than three years." Ken forgot that bet, and of course they hadn't taken him up on it anyway, but it illustrates how people's needs and desires change over time.

You can also ask how much the sellers paid, why they are selling or about anything adverse in the neighborhood. You can't guarantee honest answers, but you will hopefully get a better understanding of whether or not this is the home you want to commit to. The bottom line is that if you have a plan, and you stick to the plan and understand your limits, you will hopefully stave off buyer's remorse.

There is no way to learn everything about a home before you buy it. You can learn a lot, and we will discuss some of those things here. But the neighborhood, your neighbors, and future plans for the community are all factors you will discover over time. Your local government may decide to build a highway a few blocks away. Private enterprise may decide to put in a shopping center. Your job situation may change, or you may simply decide you would prefer living in another area for any of a variety of reasons. Very little in life is permanent. So while you may be perfectly happy with the home you choose to buy, do not be afraid to buy if everything is not perfect.

Insurance

Even if you never plan to move again, or you pay cash so there is no mortgage company making stipulations on your loan, you need to make sure the home is insurable.

Recently, a Realtor® friend reported receiving a termination notice from her insurance company. She had been insured with the same company for more than 25 years and had never filed a claim. However, the insurance company just found out that she lived more than 10 miles from a fire station.

Another Realtor® friend received a notice from one of his sellers who had recently listed a home for sale. The notice included a copy of a letter received from his insurance company. His insurance was being cancelled because his home was on the market for sale; the insurance company stated that having one's home for sale presented greater risk due to the fact that strangers will be going through it.

Any property you purchase that requires financing will also require hazard insurance, otherwise known as homeowner's insurance. Your lender will not provide financing without it. If you are purchasing a condominium, townhouse or other property that is considered a *common interest community,* this section may not apply. If the property has a homeowners' association that provides insurance on all the units, you will not have to purchase your own. Instead, you will want to get what is referred to as a "condo rider." This kind of policy is optional and similar to renters insurance in that it covers only the contents of your home and not the structure.

Insurance covers you for a number of things, the most disastrous of which being total loss of your home by fire or other calamity. Homeowner's insurance also provides you with liability coverage in the event that someone is injured on your property, and it covers you in the event of loss from theft or other smaller mishaps. Interestingly, however, some of the things that most dramatically affect homeowners are being decreased or eliminated from insurance coverage, such as coverage for mold and water leaks. As of this writing, we face a national insurance crisis.

The recurring theme of alarm in national, state and local meetings of Realtors® centers on the growing insurance crisis. More and more people are discovering that hazard insurance is hard to find or nonexistent. There are three primary reasons that insurance companies are refusing to underwrite insurance on new purchases:

1. The seller has either filed a claim, or simply called about a problem, and the insurance company no longer wishes to insure or reinsure the home. The current seller's insurance could refuse to renew or the refusal could come from a different company that has been contacted by the seller or buyer. The property may have had water problems, whether from leaky roofs, broken pipes or runoff, and the insurance company feels it may happen again or the property may have mold. The interesting thing is that the homeowner may not have even filed a claim. They may simply have called to see if a situation were covered and if they should file a claim. But overall, companies feel that properties that have experienced

past claims are more likely to experience future claims. The property now becomes, for all practical purposes, uninsurable.

2. The buyer may have had claims on a prior residence that makes the buyer, in the eyes of insurance underwriters, uninsurable. It could be because of similar problems noted above. It could be because a company had to pay a claim because the buyer's previous home was poorly maintained. Overall, companies state that buyers who have filed past claims are more likely to file future claims. Whatever the reason, the buyer becomes uninsurable.

3. The buyer may have low credit scores. What do low credit scores have to do with homeowner's insurance? Insurance companies have started to underwrite based on their assessment of a buyer's ability to properly maintain their home. In their estimation, people with low credit scores usually are unable to afford routine maintenance, leading the home to fall into disrepair and hence leading to claims-related damage.

Insurance companies claim a number of reasons for the current crisis. They point to the $40+ billion in losses in the World Trade Center terrorist attack and to major losses from natural disasters like Hurricane Katrina. They point to the surge of mold-related claims and call attention to aggressive low pricing in the past that resulted in major losses. What they do not point to, but studies have shown may be the actual reason for their loss of profits, are the losses they have suffered on their stock market investments.

The warning is clear: You can no longer take property insurance for granted. As of now, the traditional concept of automatic insurance is outdated! You must apply for and obtain homeowner's insurance at the earliest possible date in a transaction. Then, if denied by one company, there is at least time to shop for other coverage. You might also seek out an insurance broker who works with multiple lines. A broker would have a better idea of where to place an application based on either credit scores or claims history.

What Is a C.L.U.E. Report?

A claims history report on a seller's residence (called C.L.U.E. for Comprehensive Loss Underwriting Exchange) can be obtained from ChoicePoint, an online identification and credential verification service. Through their ChoiceTrust program, they manage and maintain information about claims filed on properties in the United States (www.choicetrust.com). The report will show all claims filed in the past five years, including the nature and amount of each settlement. Examples could range from water or fire damage, to even dog bites. About 90 percent of all insurers nationally participate in C.L.U.E. and a good insurance broker will most likely know those that don't.

C.L.U.E. reports are available on properties, not individuals, so when a buyer makes an offer on a property, they will have a clause requiring you to obtain a C.L.U.E. report. It will cost you approximately $20, and you can pay and download the report online or request it by mail. If you find your home is determined to be uninsurable, it's much better to know in advance so you have time to check insurability with other companies. Mortgage lenders require insurance, so if you are stuck with a property that is uninsurable, you would most likely have to attract a cash buyer to purchase the home.

Insist as a counter to any offer, that the buyer immediately contact a lender and have them check the buyer's insurance scores to make sure they are not at risk of being unable to obtain insurance (see #3 above). And once an offer becomes a contract, make sure the buyer applies for, and obtains, insurance immediately. If they have been denied coverage and received a letter from an insurance company, they can obtain a free copy of their insurance scores for review from ChoicePoint (*www.Consumer Disclosure.com.*). The point to emphasize is that you should obtain a C.L.U.E. report immediately upon listing your property for sale. Then, you will either have time to address any problems that might come up, or relax with the knowledge that there will be no concerns that could prevent a sale.

This issue of insurance has become so important that the National Association of REALTORS® has appointed an Insurance Task Force to address the growing problem. The task force has already put forth recommendations for state associations to begin working on legislation, to educate their members, and to discover other ways of handling the problem.

The Sale That Didn't Happen

One of Ken's earliest transactions involved Julie, a single mother who was selling her home and buying another. The home Julie was selling was called a "cluster home"—that is, it was located in a home project governed by a homeowners' association. It was just like a townhouse or condominium project, except the homes were detached. For Julie's soon-to-be-former home, another agent had produced a buyer and it was under contract. In addition, Ken found a home Julie wanted and put it under contract for her. Everything was going smoothly, except the lender for the buyer of Julie's former home did not get loan approval on time. Ken spoke with the lender every day and was assured the loan would be approved, even though this particular purchase was the maximum the buyer could handle. Their credit was fine and the ratios were close but acceptable, but the underwriter was overloaded, so they waited. Julie and her kids packed and scheduled a moving company.

On the day they were supposed to close on both the sale of Julie's old home and the purchase of her new home, with the house full of packed boxes and the moving van parked outside, Ken got a call from the lender. The buyer's loan had been denied. The lender hadn't noticed that there were homeowners' association dues involved with Julie's home, and didn't include that information in the loan package. Of course, he blamed Ken for not informing him of that fact, even though the information had been detailed in the contract, one of the first loan documents provided to the lender. Ken simply referred him back to that contract.

The situation was a disaster. The number of people negatively affected was enough to cause a relatively new real estate agent to quit the business before any more parties were hurt. The buyers' lease had ended and they had to move out of their apartment, now with no place to go. Julie and her two children had to stay in their old home and live out of boxes until Ken could sell it again. The sellers of the home Julie was scheduled to buy wanted to keep her earnest money because they were so angry, but Ken had the sale of Julie's home as a contingency in the contract and she got her money back. When Julie's purchase fell through, those sellers had to cancel their pending purchase of another new home. And, although less important to all of the frustrated home purchasers and sellers involved, none of the real estate agents involved in any of the transactions got paid. They all had to do their work over again.

Ken kept telling Julie through her tears that things happen for a reason, and they would get her house sold and find her an even better home to move into—which actually happened. When all was said and done, she had a far superior house to the one she would have bought, in a nicer neighborhood, closer to the schools her children would attend, and she ended up happy. But what a process getting there! We wouldn't wish that on anyone.

Therefore, we build contingencies into contracts, and we try to cover all the bases so everything that is promised actually occurs. For example, every contract should have a clause that lets you go into the home one or two days prior to closing to do a final walk-through. This lets you verify that the home is in at least as good condition as it was when you put it under contract, and that the sellers have done what they promised. For example, if your contract called for the carpets to be professionally steam cleaned (note the language—you generally don't want to settle for the sellers renting a do-it-yourself cleaner), you can make sure that was done. If certain things were to be repaired or replaced as a result of the inspection agreement, you can verify that they were.

Keep in mind that typically, nothing in the contract obligates a seller to actually clean the house for you. It is common courtesy to do so, but if that's important to you, put it in the contract. You see, contracts simply keep everything nice and tidy. If everyone you dealt with were completely honest, had an impeccable memory, and always had it in their heart to do the right thing, contracts probably wouldn't be necessary. But even honest people have short memories, or get in a hurry, or decide they've already given too much, which makes contracts a valuable necessity.

Bring your Realtor® with you on your walk-through. Bring to the listing agent's attention anything that wasn't completed according to the contract, and have it corrected prior to closing. Ultimately, you hold the trump card: You have the money to hand over at the closing table, and if your agreement hasn't been honored, you can decline to close. Practically speaking, that rarely happens when everything is in place to close. You've probably packed or otherwise made plans to move out of your current residence, you are excited about being in a new home, and the pressure is on everyone to go ahead and sign. So again, don't sweat the small stuff.

Anything significant should be handled with a written agreement at closing, or by setting aside additional money in escrow. For example, let's say the seller was to replace the furnace but couldn't arrange for a repairperson in time. You could all agree to have the title company or escrow company withhold that money from the proceeds due to be paid to the seller. The title or escrow company would then pay the repairperson when the work was complete. Or if the carpet was supposed to be cleaned but wasn't, the seller could hand you a check at closing to pay for it.

What do you do if the seller refuses? You have to make a decision. Is it more important to close, or should you walk away? We're not telling you this because it happens often, but because it does happen occasionally, it's best to be prepared.

If your transaction is typical, everything will have been completed per agreement and you'll sign the closing papers, present your check, and get the keys to the house. Everybody walks away with big grins on their faces, looking forward to the new lives they have created.

Now for the fun part—it's time to move in to your new home!

To Reach Susan Mekenney
Mail: 5213 Concordia Street
Fairfax, VA 22032
Phone: (800)768-8650
www.movetovirginia.com
susan@movetovirginia.com

To Reach Ken Deshaies:
Mail: P.O. Box 37
330 Dillion Ridge Road, Suite 6
Dillon, CO 80435
Phone: (888) 221-7669 or (970) 262-7669
Fax: (866) 782-6059
www.SnowHome.com
www.BuyerAgency.net
Ken@SnowHome.com

APPENDIX A

Moving Checklist

8 Weeks Before Moving:

- ❑ Create a "move file" to keep track of estimates, receipts and other important information.
- ❑ Check with the IRS to see what expenses can be deducted on your next tax return.
- ❑ Start pulling together medical and dental records and ask your health care providers for referrals in your new city.
- ❑ Start researching your new community. The Internet is a great resource for finding chambers of commerce and community guides.
- ❑ Get estimates from several moving companies and compare them.
- ❑ Arrange to have school records transferred to your children's new school.

6 Weeks Before Moving:

- ❑ Make a list of things that are valuable or difficult to replace. Plan on shipping these by certified mail or carrying them with you.
- ❑ Start working your way through each room taking inventory and planning what to get rid of. Start planning a yard sale and find local charities.
- ❑ Choose a moving company and reserve the date of your move.
- ❑ Start collecting boxes and other packing supplies.
- ❑ Check how to obtain new driver's licenses and license plates.

4 Weeks Before Moving:

- ❑ Send out change of address cards to post office, friends, subscriptions and credit cards.
- ❑ Hold your garage sale. Donate left over items to charity.
- ❑ Contact utility companies and notify them of disconnect dates. Arrange for utility service in your new home.
- ❑ Start packing items you don't use often.

2 Weeks Before Moving:

- ❑ Contact your bank and/or credit union to transfer or close accounts. Clear out safety deposit boxes.
- ❑ Confirm travel and moving arrangements.
- ❑ Return library books or anything borrowed from friends or neighbors.

1 Week Before Moving:

- ❑ Finish packing! Separate essential items that you will be taking with you.
- ❑ Empty, defrost and clean your refrigerator at least 24 hours prior to moving day.
- ❑ Cancel deliveries and services such as newspapers and trash collection.
- ❑ Drain oil and gasoline from power equipment.

Moving Day:

- ❑ Before the movers leave, check every room, closet and cabinet one last time.

- ❑ Upon arriving, inspect everything and make sure nothing was damaged during the move.
- ❑ Keep all moving receipts and documentation in your file.

After the Move:

- ❑ If needed, childproof your new home.
- ❑ Test security and smoke alarms.
- ❑ Set up all appliances.
- ❑ Get local emergency numbers and post them.
- ❑ Change the locks on all doors.
- ❑ Explore your new neighborhood!

APPENDIX B

Home Preparation Checklist

Step 1: Make Any Needed Repairs to the Primary Systems and Components of Your Home

(Unless you are selling your home "as is", buyers will need to know that your home's systems are in working order. If they are not, you should make the repairs before putting your home on the market unless you want to compensate the buyer monetarily. Take a thorough inventory and inspection of the following systems and components of your home to make sure that they are in working order. While these repairs might be costly, it will usually save you money to take care of them now rather than crediting the buyer at closing. These are items that you need to repair before you do anything else to your home if you can handle the expense).

- ❑ Make sure that your roof is in good repair. If your home has been experiencing any leaks, your roof might need to be replaced. If any shingles are loose or broken, they need to be replaced.

- ❑ Check to see that your rain gutters are flowing properly and in the right direction and are free of leaves and dirt.

- ❑ Your heating and air conditioning should be in good working order. If they are not, this can definitely cause problems in finding buyers for your house.

- ❑ Make sure that your house is structurally sound. Any cracks in the walls or ceilings should be filled in immediately to avoid further cracking.

- ❑ Check that all plumbing and septic systems are working as they should. If they are not, call in a plumber or other specialists as needed.

- ❑ Check your house for termites or any other pests. If you find any, call in a specialist to get rid of them!

- ❑ If your home has mold you should take care of it unless you are willing to sell your home for less or possibly not even find a buyer.
- ❑ Check your home for flood damage if you live in an area where flooding could be a problem.
- ❑ Radon and lead paint are serious problems that you should check for. It is best to know now rather than be surprised later on and have a deal fall through.
- ❑ If you have any broken windows, window panes, screens or doors, you should pay to have them fixed.
- ❑ If you have any broken appliances that are fixtures and therefore will be included in the sale, such as the dishwasher, you should pay to have them fixed or replaced. Likewise, repair any broken light fixtures.
- ❑ If you have a gas stove, make sure that it works properly and that there are no gas leaks.
- ❑ Make sure all electrical systems are working properly. This includes any electrical gates, garage, doorbell, intercom, and so on.
- ❑ If there are any dead or "sick" trees on your property, have them cut down.

Step 2: The Exterior of Your Home

(The exterior of your house is the first thing a potential buyer will see as they approach. Make sure that it looks neat and cared for. Use the following checklist as a guide.)

- ❑ Your lawn should be mowed and well trimmed. An overgrown lawn can be a big turn off to potential buyers and can really detract their attention from other aspects of your home.

- ❑ Your lawn should also be green and not brown. Fertilize it if necessary and remember to keep it free of weeds.
- ❑ Shrubs, flowers, trees and bushes should be well trimmed and healthy looking. Let buyers know that you care for your home lovingly. Well cared for greenery can give your home much added appeal.
- ❑ If you have fruit trees, make sure to get rid of any rotting fruit that has fallen to the ground.
- ❑ Rake your lawn and front drive free of drifting leaves.
- ❑ Make sure that your front walk, lawn and entryway are clear of clutter. Get rid of any toys or bikes and store them properly.
- ❑ Hose down your front entryway so it is clean and free of dirt. If it is stained, think about covering the stain with a nice doormat if it can't be cleaned.
- ❑ If your driveway has any oil stains, clean them. Oil stains can really be an eye sore.
- ❑ If your front door looks old or worn, give it a fresh coat of paint or polish it.
- ❑ Think about placing some potted flowers by your front door. Flowers always look pretty and smell sweet.
- ❑ Wash your windows!
- ❑ If you haven't painted your house in some time and it is looking a bit shabby, you might want to consider painting it, but try to stay away from bold colors.
- ❑ Fix or replace any broken shutters, shingles or bricks.

Step 3: The Interior of Your Home

(Most of the steps taken here will be more time intensive than anything else so follow these steps to make the inside of your home attractive and inviting).

- ❑ Organize and minimize everything in your home from top to bottom. This will involve going through every room, closet, cabinet and any other storage area such as the garage and clearing out your belongings. You want to let potential buyers see as much clear space as possible so this is the time to get rid of anything you no longer want or need and store the rest of your belongings neatly. You will have to do this eventually when you move, so why not start now in order to help give your home some added appeal to potential buyers? If you have so much stuff that you don't know what to do with it all, consider storing it with family or friends or perhaps renting storage space.

- ❑ Make sure that your house is clean and tidy. Clean everything in your house inside and out. Wax the floors, make sure the walls are free of dirt and smudges and dust and vacuum your furniture.

- ❑ Go through every room in your house and make sure that the furniture is arranged to make the room look the most spacious and aesthetically pleasing. Enlist the opinions of others. If you have torn, broken, very worn out or dirty furniture, you should get rid of it if you plan to do so anyway. If you can't, try covering the furniture. For example, a nice afghan over an old couch can do the trick.

- ❑ Make sure that the parts of your home that you like best are getting good lighting. Make sure that the windows are unobstructed to let in the sunlight and keep the curtains or blinds open.

- ❑ Wash the windows so they are completely clear. If any window coverings are worn or broken, fix or replace them.
- ❑ Make sure that all of your lights are working. Replace burned-out bulbs, but make sure to keep the lighting inviting.
- ❑ Clean your kitchen counters and tile so they sparkle and clean the sink. Kitchens are very important to buyers so make sure that yours is clean and bright. The kitchen is also a great place to place fresh flowers.
- ❑ Clean everything in the bathroom until it shines. Get rid of any rust stains. Hang fresh, clean towels neatly.
- ❑ Air out your house to get rid of any bad or stale odors. Try to bring in some fresh scents with flowers or a touch of vanilla.

Step 4: Updating Your Home

(If you have the time and the money, there are certain things that you can do to your home to give it added appeal and a much better selling price. There are certain things that buyers look for when buying a home, so if you do have the means, consider the following projects if they are needed).

- ❑ Remodels and updates in the kitchen are where you can get the greatest returns on your investment when you sell your home. If your kitchen is outdated and you have the means, certain updates can greatly improve your chances at selling your home for a better price.
- ❑ If your appliances are over 10 years old, replace them with new, modern appliances. Stainless steel appliances are the latest trends today.

- ❑ Old cabinets and countertops can also be replaced. If you are handy, this can even be a do-it-yourself project. Natural woods for the cabinets and granite or tile countertops can make your kitchen sparkle.
- ❑ Old linoleum flooring in the kitchen can really make the room look dingy. Consider replacing with hardwood or even tile.
- ❑ After the kitchen, updates in the bathroom are where you will see a good return on your investment in the sale price of your home. Buyers today are looking for modern bathrooms with all the latest conveniences. Glass shower doors, new tiles, flooring and new fixtures can all give your bathrooms an entirely new look.
- ❑ If your walls are looking dirty and old, a new paint job can do wonders to the look of the inside of your home. This can be an inexpensive project that can really brighten up the rooms of your house. Choose neutral colors for a warm and soft look that will appeal to the greatest number of buyers.
- ❑ If your floors are worn and dirty, consider replacing them. Old and worn carpeting can really detract a buyer's attention from other features of your home. New carpeting can be relatively inexpensive compared with the greater return that can be obtained in the selling price of your home.
- ❑ Outdated flooring such as linoleum can make your house look retro. Most buyers are looking for homes with modern updates. If you can't afford hardwood, consider vinyl.
- ❑ Other areas to consider are very old windows and doors. Windows encompass a great deal of your

home's exterior and are definitely something that buyers will notice right away.

Congratulations, after having followed these steps and preparing your house so that it looks its best, you are now ready to sell your home!

Notes

Notes

Ordering Information

Regarding the REALTOR® titles, we have many different editions for home buyers *and* home sellers across the country. Even though they may be location-specific due to different area laws, the concepts still hold true.

If you would like a title from our buyer book series in your area, *How to Make Your REALTOR® Get You the Best Deal*, please see current editions at our buyers agency web site: www.BuyerAgency.net. All buyer agency books are priced at **$17.95** each.

If you would like a copy of our seller book series for your area, *Get the Best Deal When Selling Your Home*, please visit our web site at: www.GabrielBooks.com for current editions. All seller books are priced at **$18.95** each.

For additional information, please call (800) 940-2622.

Additional Books for Personal, Financial and Business Growth:

Couples and Money, by Victoria Collins, PhD $13.95

This is a vital guide for supporting couples to thrive financially and emotionally. It provides exercises and instructions in order to help couples talk about money. Recommended by Consumer Credit Counseling Service.

Wealth On Any Income, by Rennie Gabriel,
CLU, CFP, UCLA Instructor $17.95

Move from creating financial goals to achieving them. This book covers both the emotional and practical aspects of handling money effectively, and how to move from debt to wealth on any income. Endorsed by Mark Victor Hansen, co-author of the *Chicken Soup for the Soul®* series.

Wealth On Any Income cassette tape program,
by Rennie Gabriel $59.00

A comprehensive but simple-to-use program teaching anyone to handle money effectively, get out of debt, live within their income and begin investing with as little as $100. This is an instructional guide to ultimately creating financial independence. Includes the above book and two spending registers. Five hours read by Rennie Gabriel, the author.

Money Talk, by Todd Rainey $17.95

A gay and lesbian guide to financial success, including partnership agreements and health care powers.

How to Outwit and Outsell Your Competition,
by Shirley Lee $14.95

Grow your business 50–200% per year using little-known, powerful strategies that cannot fail. Avoid costly marketing blunders by learning from common mistakes.

Hollywood Beauty Secrets, by Louisa Maccan-Graves $21.95

Women don't have to spend a fortune to be their very best. Author and top hands and parts model, Louisa Maccan-Graves lists affordable, effective products and rejuvenating therapies that slow down and even reverse aging. These products ignite fat burning, balance hormones, diminish deep wrinkles and frown lines, relieve depression and decrease body fat without prescription drugs, plastic surgery or invasive procedures. Louisa also reveals effective beauty recipes that can be made using household ingredients. Packed with intelligent advice and anti-aging breakthroughs, there is something here for every woman.

Roller Hockey, The Game Within the Game,
by Warren R. Taylor. $19.95

If you play roller hockey, this book has valuable lessons that will help take your game to the highest level. If you are a coach, the diagrams in this book will assist you in teaching the game and help you build a powerful, winning team. If you are a parent or fan, this book will increase your understanding and passion for the game.

Hearing Voices, Creating Voicing & Producing Great Radio Commercials, by Alan Barzman $19.95

An amusing and informative examination of what it takes to create and produce highly effective and humorous radio commercials by a multiple award-winning producer and voice-over artist.

The 50+ Boomer, by Donald L. Potter $19.95

The 50+ Boomers are the biggest spending, and most under-marketed-to, group of consumers in history. Nationally known lecturer and author Don Potter explains the rewards awaiting those marketers who are ready to engage this vital demographic. This book provides the road-map on how to reach this group and motivate them to buy.

To order books by Gabriel Publications,
visit our web site at: www.GabrielBooks.com,
e-mail us at: info@GabrielBooks.com
or call us at (800) 940-COACH (940-2622)